Jesus, Dollars and Sense

Jesus, Dollars and Sense

*An Effective
Stewardship Guide
for Clergy and Lay Leaders*

Foreword by

Furman C. Stough

EPISCOPAL BISHOP OF ALABAMA

Edited by Oscar C. Carr, Jr.

The Seabury Press • A CROSSROAD BOOK • *New York*

The Seabury Press
815 Second Avenue
New York, N.Y. 10017

Printed in the United States of America

Library of Congress Cataloging in Publication Data

Main entry under title:

Jesus, dollars and sense.

"A Crossroad book."

1. Stewardship, Christian—Addresses, essays, lectures. 2. Stewardship, Christian—Sermons. 3. Protestant Episcopal Church in the U.S.A.—Sermons. 4. Sermons, American. I. Title.

BV772.J45   248'.6   76-14362

ISBN 0-8164-2132-3

Contents

PART THREE

Selected Sermons

When Sylvia Green Wilks died in New York on February 5, 1951, the terms of her will, probated eleven months later, made her the most generous benefactor to Episcopal causes in the history of the Church. The tall, austere recluse—virtually unknown except as the daughter of Hetty Green (1834–1916)—spent the last of her eighty years in an apartment at 988 Fifth Avenue.

On January 31, 1952, the Chase National Bank mailed the checks to the long list of recipients. For almost all of them, the windfall was totally unexpected. A majority had never seen Mrs. Wilks. In some cases the news reporters, to whom the bank had released the details on the same day, arrived at the parish, hospital, or person's home before the check.

Receiving one share each (approximately $650,000) were two New York City churches: St. Bartholomew's and St. George's. Others with one share each were Christ Church, Greenwich, Conn.; Immanuel, Bellows Falls, Vt.; St. Ann's, Brooklyn, N. Y.; Trinity, Newport, R.I.; and Seamen's Church Institute in New York City.

Two shares were received by St. James, Hyde Park, N. Y. (the Franklin Delano Roosevelt parish); St. Peter's, Morristown, N. J.; Incarnation, Trinity, and General Seminary, New York City; and St. Luke's Hospital, New Bedford, Mass.

The largest beneficiaries, with four shares each, included five Episcopal institutions: St. Luke's Home for Aged Women and St. Luke's Hospital in New York; Kent School in Connecticut; Groton School in Massachusetts; and St. Paul's School in New Hampshire. These five bequests were worth slightly more than $2.5 million each.

The source of the Wilks fortune went back to the shipping days in New England when her forebears, the Howland and Robinson families sent whalers into the Atlantic and merchant ships to China.

It is worthy of note that Sylvia Wilks's interest in the Episcopal Church dated from the private schooling she received in the parish school of Immanuel Church, Bellows Falls, Vermont. She probably attended, at least once, every parish she enriched, but most of the rectors who shared her final largesse admitted that they would not have recognized her. The most generous testator in Episcopal Church history was a lonely woman who probably needed more of her Church's ministry than she received.

We joyfully dedicate this book to her memory in the hope that her generous example will inspire others.

Foreword

I believe it was Archbishop Temple who said: "Mission is to the Church as flame is to a fire." There are now many Episcopalians who could paraphrase that comment and say, "Stewardship is to a Christian as flame is to a fire."

For the first time in our era, the stewardship of money is being talked about openly and without apology in our Church; tithing is no longer a taboo subject. We are constantly encountering lay people, priests, and bishops who are tithers, and who have thus found some of the deep joy of the Gospel and a sense of freedom in the Christian life that they had never known before.

Much of this new impetus has come from the Office of Development of the Episcopal Church and its executive, Dr. Oscar C. Carr. Under his leadership, stewardship resources scattered throughout our Church have been brought together and made available to all of us through provincial seminars and workshops. At times, he alone, through his own imagination and initiative, has kept this Church face-forward to its responsibility and potential as a good steward of its financial resources.

Coupled with this has been the Presiding Bishop's constant call for our Church to break out of old patterns of funding, thereby giving our dioceses, parishes, and communicants many and varied ways to express their understanding of the stewardship of money.

In this book you will find some of the soundest and most workable theology and methodology in the Episcopal Church today as it relates to the stewardship of money. We know that it is viable because we have experienced some of the joy and excitement that comes when Christian men and women are able to grasp a New Testament perspective on money.

Some years back it was my dear friend of long standing, Gert Behanna, who began to turn me in the direction of a more meaningful life that included a stewardship of money based on a very simple two-point theology—namely, all the money we have or that there is in the world belongs to God anyhow; and, the best thing a Christian can do with money is to keep it moving.

Furman C. Stough
BISHOP OF ALABAMA

Introduction

"We can never ransom ourselves or deliver to God the price of our life; for the ransom of our life is so great that we should never have enough to pay it." So wrote the psalmist in the Forty-ninth Psalm long, long before the time of Jesus.

Where your treasure is, there will your heart be also.
Jesus of Nazareth

To separate the essential from the nonessential is what I call being spiritual.
Franz Marc

The truth shall make you free—but first it shall make you miserable!
Old Proverb

It was not the least bit surprising that the highly professional, intelligent, and concerned publishers of Seabury Press first objected to my suggestion of *Jesus, Dollars and Sense* as the title for this book! That objection was most significant and understandable. The word juxtaposition in the title is the medium for the message, because this is a book about money as a sacramental expression of the Christian believer.

If this makes us uncomfortable—and it usually does because of our conditioning—it is because we are not aware of the recorded approach of Jesus to the subject of man's relationship to his money. Many people are indeed surprised to discover that Jesus understood, as well as any person who ever lived, the deep and compelling potential for good or evil that exists in the relationship of a person to his money. Many people believe Jesus talked most about peace and forgiveness and prayer and sacrifice and the kingdom of God. This is not true. As recorded in the New Testament, Jesus talked most about the relationship of a person and his material possessions. One sixth of all the words of Jesus are concerned

with this one subject. One third of all Jesus' parables are de-
voted to it. Money, and what it represents to us, has been a
major preoccupation of every generation, and I submit—for
Jesus' sake—that the Church should not treat discussions
about money as if money were a bad "four-letter" word. On
the contrary, relationships in regard to money should have
the same high priority in every Church's program of education that Jesus places on it. All year round, for all age groups,
starting in the pulpit, we should be made ever mindful of the
relationship of a person to his material possessions.

At the very outset, I want to establish different definitions
for fund raising and for Christian stewardship. Fund raising
means getting people to give more money. Christian stewardship helps people to be more giving. Christian stewardship could be defined as the effective commitment or invest-
ment of human and material resources in participation with
Christ in his love for others.

Before dealing with the history of how this book came into
being, I want to make some major points about stewardship
as developed for the most part by Bob Cooper, our "traveling
stewardship theologian." There are two primary points of
equal importance. The first point is that stewardship always
has to do with a Christian's task of giving away gifts that have
already been given to him by God. This presupposes, of
course, acceptance of the belief that all things are conferred
on us by God. The second point is that stewardship always
has to do with a Christian getting free of what binds him. In
our culture, nothing binds us more than money—the symbol
of material things. The first point has to do with turning to a
new life; the latter with turning away from an old life. In
other words, stewardship is intimately and inextricably intertwined with conversion. One has to be turned away from
slavery or, to say it another way, converted from what binds
him. Conversely, one must turn toward what frees him,
namely, the task of giving away what God has given him.
This is the test of conversion.

The task of stewardship is stewardship of the Gospel.
Those who think or teach that stewardship has primarily to

do with fund raising, or having only to do with money for that matter, present a caricature. They don't pass the test of defining the task. Evangelism can never be primary in the sense that it takes precedence over the stewardship of the Gospel, which is the Church's first obligation. Evangelism is one strategy for giving away the Good News that God has acted finally and definitively in Christ to free man from himself. Evangelism, as it is talked about in the Episcopal Church, is too frequently aimed at the Church itself. That is an incredible and curious notion, because it is an indictment of our own bondage—an indication of our own lack of freedom. The Good News (evangelism) is then not really good news, because the institutional Church, like the world, is preoccupied with its own agenda—with having its own way against God. The Church as an institution is a kind of slave that loves its own bonds. Evangelism must still be understood to entail the necessity of getting free of what is our major bond, namely, our preoccupation with money and with the things that money will buy.

The principal task of evangelization, like the principal task of stewardship, is that of bearing the Good News to the world. This is simply another way of stating that the principal task of stewardship is the stewardship of the Gospel. There is ample biblical warrant for this. I limit my remarks to three instances. Evangelism, like stewardship, has to have a mind in order to have a strategy. The biblical warrant for this can be found in Jesus' particular prescription for the rich young ruler. To him Jesus says he has to sell everything he has and give it to the poor. This is not for everyone, of course. This was a particular thing—riches—that enslaved this particular person. This particular person needed to be free from the thing that bound him the most—his material possessions. Evangelism has to be particular. Stewardship has to be particular. By particularity, I mean a specific opportunity is shown to a particular person whose circumstances are highly specific.

A second biblical piece of material which supports the essential point here—that evangelism is primarily stewardship of the Gospel—is from Paul's second letter to the church in Corinth. In the fourth chapter, Paul is speaking about "this ministry," the ministry of the Gospel, which is the treasure we have "in earthen vessels."

A third instance of biblical support for this view is found in the Epistle of James. In that epistle the writer heaps scorn upon the notion of a work-less faith. In the Episcopal Church one can find two extremes which are both caricatures of a view James holds. Among some Anglo-Catholics the faith really has to do with the old cliché of "Mass, Mary, and Confession." It is too easily believed by some that if one simply does these things and does them unrelentingly, then one's obligation of stewardship or evangelism has been fulfilled. Some evangelicals, on the other hand, too frequently assume that "gospelizing" is all that is necessary in order to carry out their task. In both of these extreme examples one is apt to find an absence of significant giving of money. Neither of these extreme positions pass my definition of the test of conversion, the stewardship of the Gospel.

I have some concern—or prejudice, if you will—developed over the years along the sawdust trails of the Bible Belt, that evangelism is often seized upon as a panacea. When things are bad for the Church we say, "If only we did our primary job of evangelizing, then we would be able to cure our greatest ills." With appropriate changes, the same sort of thing could be said of the Anglo-Catholic extremists who believe that if Mass and Confession become primary in the life of a person, then the Church's ills would most surely be on the road to healing. I submit that if the Church's ills were ever to be cured, its membership must pass the test of conversion embraced in full stewardship of the Gospel. The best and most precise definition of the scope of the stewardship of which I speak is: the ordering of one's life so that the Gospel of Christ may be shared with all men and women.

I think you would agree that we as a Church are not where we would like to be.

No matter what we hope to be, do, or become, the only place to start is with where we are. We are no other place. In order to know really where we are, however, we must know really where we have been—where we have come from. In the matter of stewardship concerns, as we approach the Minnesota General Convention, it will be helpful to reflect on stewardship concerns at the time of the 64th General Convention in Louisville, Kentucky, three years ago.

In the months leading up to that convention, the Executive Council felt that the Church should address itself to the need for a national, multimillion dollar, renewal fund campaign to relieve the pain of not being able to respond to the multitude of mission opportunities that abound. The Office of Development and the Executive Council went to the convention prepared to suggest and recommend such an effort. We had secured pledges from Trinity Parish in New York and the Episcopal Church Foundation to launch the drive. At the last minute, the Executive Council postponed the idea for such a campaign. One of the main reasons for doing so was the negative response from the House of Deputies' Committee on Stewardship when the idea was tested with them. (I think it is worthy of note that the House of Bishops does not have a Committee on Stewardship.)

I'll never forget the response of the stewardship committee following our presentation. They didn't want to consider seriously a major national campaign—or even talk about it. They weren't hostile; they just felt our timing was bad, that the cart was before the horse. In retrospect, we can see that they were dead right. They said their first need was for stewardship help at the parish level. They acknowledged that there were excellent textbooks on the market covering the very specific work of fund raising and organizational development, but that for the most part they were technical, dry, unexciting, nonstimulating. They recalled the "Chicago 101" report that showed the great lack of knowledge at the parish level, even about diocesan programs, much less about programs of the Church at the national and international levels, and how they all relate. The committee observed that the purpose of a development office is to develop and implement a strategy that will increase the financial resources of the Church. They felt that the first phase of any long-range development strategy—undergirding any major national fund drive in the future—should be a solid Christian stewardship program for the Church. That program should provide skill and training workshops, quality Every Member Visitation materials, audiovisual and linear resources, and regional consultants for parishes and dioceses that might need or request them. We listened. More important, we heard. We went to work to implement that primary phase.

The priority for stewardship resource development on the Episcopal Church Center staff had been very low. We found, for instance, the last book on stewardship published by The Seabury Press—*Tall in His Presence* by Canon George McNeill Ray of Trinity Cathedral, Phoenix, Arizona—was published in 1961. So we started almost from scratch. The results of our efforts have been extraordinary. We are grateful to all the committed and talented church men and women who made the success possible. This book records part of that success story.

Between December 1974 and May 1976—a period of only seventeen months—with a limited Office of Development staff at the Episcopal Church Center, we conducted nine provincial stewardship workshops in Dallas, Texas; Albany, New York; Laramie, Wyoming; Portland, Oregon; Phoenix, Arizona; Jacksonville, Florida; Washington, D.C.; South Attleboro, Massachusetts; and Chicago, Illinois. These workshops were well attended and very well received. The one thousand participants who rated the workshops on personal evaluation sheets gave them the highest ratings for both substance and form that I have ever seen in my life in the Church.

Ninety-four percent of all respondents gave the workshops a rating of eighty percent or better, and two thirds rated the workshops one hundred percent effective!

Some of the comments were interesting:

> Good movement—good sharing—vindicates switchboard procedure.
>
> The Rt. Rev. Lloyd Gressle
> Bishop of Bethlehem (Pa.)

More design and help for smaller congregations—some kind of workshop for missions and small parishes.

> The Rev. William Todd
> West Virginia

The whole Church needs this help!

> The Rt. Rev. G. Edward Haynsworth
> Bishop of Nicaragua

It was a pleasure to see a well-run workshop—fast, condensed, and informative.

> Mr. Stanley Harbor
> Arizona

A first rate group of leaders—balanced, attractive, good communicators. Right on!

> The Rev. John Cannon
> New York

My only regret is that I did not urge more people from our diocese to come.

> The Rev. Canon Henry Biggin
> Newark

Need lay people—a woman—on the program.

> Ms. Elizabeth Workman
> Mississippi

Too bad more promotion of workshop was not given by my diocese.

> The Rev. Lee Graham, Jr.
> Florida

They are all tops. Variety and yet unity.

> The Rev. Frank A. Smith
> Southeast Florida

Knew nothing of stewardship before I came—found this tremendously helpful.

> The Rev. Edward C. Chapman
> Georgia

Balance and interplay between leaders exceptional. Differences between models give plenty of building materials for typical parish.

> Henry L. McCorkle
> Editor, *Episcopalian*, Pennsylvania

All speakers were excellent!
> Frank M. Floyd,
> Stewardship Advisor to Diocese
> of Chicago

As good a schedule and format as can be imagined. I am very impressed!
> The Rt. Rev. Frederick Belden
> Bishop of Rhode Island

Then it (the Holy Spirit?) hit me. *I* was being addressed and challenged. Did *I* really *believe* all that I was being asked to believe. I want you to know you are succeeding in your stewardship program with this Episcopalian!
> Mrs. Emily Stramese
> Western Massachusetts

Having participated in many workshops and conferences both as a participant and as a leader, this is one of the best run and most productive I've been to.
> The Rt. Rev. Frederick B. Wolf
> Bishop of Maine and
> President of Province I

Those program leaders were:

The Very Rev. J. C. Michael Allen, D.D., Dean, Berkeley Divinity School at Yale; Associate Dean, Yale Divinity School.

The Rev. Robert M. Cooper, D.Div., Professor of Ethics and Moral Theology, Nashotah House.

The Rev. Canon H. Ebert Hobbs, Administrative Assistant to the Bishop of Ohio.

The Rev. John H. MacNaughton, Rector, Christ Church, San Antonio; former Stewardship Chairman, Diocese of Minnesota.

The Rev. George F. Regas, Rel.D., Rector, All Saints' Church, Pasadena, California.

The Rev. James L. Sanders, Rector, St. Paul's Church, Selma, Alabama.

The Rt. Rev. Furman C. Stough, D.D., Bishop of Alabama.

Ashley Hale, Congregational Development Center, Laguna Hills, California.

The Church at large and this office in particular are in their debt. We are also grateful to Trinity Parish of New York and the Episcopal Church Foundation for making these workshops possible.

The theological papers of Dean Allen and Dr. Cooper undergirded the discussions on methodology. Although the approaches to stewardship methodology vary, they all support a common goal and all are theologically sound. We do not want even to suggest that this book contains some revolutionary new concepts that will miraculously get us "off the financial hook." I see the book as an evolutionary contribution. Evolution takes place when something more is added to what has been. Development occurs when we build on the past—not when we destroy it. This book is an attempt in that direction, part of an augmentative process, with more to come.

In addition to the provincial workshops, the Office of Development has conducted diocesan workshops and assisted parishes with their stewardship concerns. We will continue to do so upon request. The office maintains a list of regional consultants available for parish or diocesan consultation. We stock audiovisual and stewardship resource materials of the highest quality. The Every Member Visitation materials continue to improve in quality and variety. We invite your comments, queries, suggestions, and constructive criticism.

I am personally grateful to the Presiding Bishop for his belief in and support of a strong stewardship program. I am indebted to Dr. John B. Coburn, Chairman of the Executive Council Committee on Development, and to the Development Committee members, for their counsel and advice. I give thanks for the guidance over the years from our national Advisory Committee on Development. And lastly, I give very special thanks to my assistant, Cathy Morphet, for the superb job of arranging the provincial workshops; and for everything that my associate, Dick Anderson, does—including putting together the pieces of this book.

One of the greatest stewards our Church has ever known is our retired Presiding Bishop, the Rt. Rev. Henry Knox Sherill. What he once said is an inspiring note on which to conclude—and on which to begin!

"When one stops to consider the world in which we live with the great amount of suffering, of hatred, and with the threat of war, the magnitude of the task becomes apparent.

We are to do our best to make the kingdoms of this world the kingdom of God and of his Christ. This task demands all that we are and all that we have. God grant to us all greater vision, more capacity to give and to serve in this the greatest of all undertakings."

New York, N.Y.   Oscar C. Carr, Jr.
August 4, 1976

PART ONE
Theology

Robert M. Cooper

Anyone who had a stereotyped image of Nashotah House would have it shattered after hearing Professor Bob Cooper (Ethics and Moral Theology) talk for three minutes. Bob's homespun analogies, understandable theology, sense of humor, and ability to poke fun at himself made him a "super-star" wherever he spoke as our "traveling stewardship theologian." Bob holds five degrees: Catawba College, Berkeley Divinity School, University of the South, Louisiana State University, and a doctorate from Vanderbilt University. This does not prevent him, however, from talking about his "Bill Cosby theory" or his admiration for the quality of George Dickel whiskey. Bob receives great joy from his efforts as priest-in-charge of a mission church and finds his work as an editor of the Anglican Theological Review *most rewarding. I don't feel that it's much of a risk to prophesy that we'll be hearing a lot more from and about him as he continues to serve the Lord and preach the Gospel in pulpit, club, and seminary classroom.*

Gift and Freedom: A Biblical Basis for Stewardship

IT IS APPROPRIATE to speak of "a biblical basis for stewardship" if for no other reason than because it is deeply Christian and Anglican to do so. I do not intend to dwell on many spe-

cific texts (so-called "proof texts"), but rather on the broad
themes of the Bible as they are pertinent to stewardship. It is
never adequate—and this needs to be said firmly and finally
at the outset—just to assume that the biblical testimony alone
is proof of how we, in our time, ought to behave. The Bible is
already theology. It is the record, among other things, of the
response of persons to God. The Bible is a basis of understanding the *meaning* of things, the very meaning of our lives.
Having said as much, I am led directly to make the first main
point I wish to put forth.

All worth is conferred upon us. "And God saw all that he had
made, and behold! it was very good." Christians are people
who have begun to realize how much they are worth. The
Old Testament tells us that the world is made by God, and
that it is good. Would we ever have concluded from the evidence of our senses that the world is, in fact, good? Would
we, that is, conclude from what we continually see and hear
of the state of the world that it is good? that people are good?
The evidence is mixed. We are told that we are good because
the world is good and we are part of the world. That knowledge of the world's goodness is itself a gift.

The New Testament tells us that God has shown us how
much we are worth, and shown us humanly and directly, by
showing us how much we are loved: "While we were yet sin-
ners Christ died for the ungodly." We have been shown it, we
have been told it; and still we only partly believe it.

The task of stewardship is to build on that "partly believing." Our task in the Church is always that of building on,
and with, what we already have. That can be put better: Our
task is that of building on, and with, what we already have.
That can be put better: Our task is that of building on *what we
already are.* We are reconciled to God and to each other, and
that is done by the gift of Christ. We are to be stewards of reconciliation. After all, the steward's task is to look out for
what he has been given.

It is clear that the steward is not a hoarder or a narrowly
custodial functionary. He is to multiply that with which he is
entrusted; he is to multiply the gift. That word "gift" is the
crucial word, and the central action in the theme of these re-

marks. More precisely, then, the task of being a steward comes down to dealing with gifts.

Gifts are difficult—the most difficult—things for us to deal with. This is so because *to accept a gift is to admit a need.* And along with that—as if that alone were not enough of a task—we come to understand ourselves as having a *need to give.* To accept a gift is at least tacitly to admit that I can, in fact, be given something by someone—by someone, that is, outside myself. It is always the implicit admission that I am not adequate to myself.

It is reported by Paul, in the Acts of the Apostles, that Jesus said, "It is more blessed to give than to receive." Yes. Surely. But it is more difficult to receive than it is to give. One task of Christian stewardship is to multiply the capacity for receiving. Being a giver can be a deadly and dangerous thing: Giving can be a vehicle for pride and supposed self-sufficiency; the giver is too easily a controller (of others). There is some help for us here in a couple of German words: *Gabe* and *Aufgabe,* "gift" and "task." Every gift carries with it a task. The steward knows that.

The first task is, as we have seen, that of accepting or receiving a gift. That can be a difficulty for stewards. What are we to do with the gifts? Hoard them? Narrowly protect them? Take no risks with them? No so! We receive in order to give away. *Gifts are to be used.* This is true in every case I can think of, even of so-called beautiful "nonutilitarian" gifts. The use of such gifts consists in admiration, in aesthetic appreciation. Some gifts embarrass us. What are we to do with *that?* Such gifts scandalize us. They constitute an *embarras de richesses.* Jesus himself is such an unwanted gift. That is why Paul, in his letter to Corinth, calls him a scandal, a stumbling block. There are a variety of responses to such gifts. Among the responses are these: I am not worthy. What does he want in return? (Yes. A gift carries with it a task.) What do I do with *this?* After all, I deserve it.

Now gifts, by definition, are not *earned.* Wages are earned; they constitute a kind of obligation. But we must be careful here, for to receive a gift is to become obligated: obligated to use it, to give it away. In a no-strings-attached culture like ours this is itself a scandal. Ours is a culture that increasingly seeks conditions where there are no binding ties, a culture that seeks ephemeral relationships. The whole of our culture tends now toward being an agglomeration of one-night stands, a culture of best sellers.

I have asserted so far that there are two things to be done with gifts received: first, we are to use them; and second, we are to use them by giving them away. Let the receiver give. I have now a third thing to say about giving and receiving. The recipient of a *gift*, that is the receiver of something un-earned, is typically *grateful*. "Grateful" is related to the word *gratis*, to the word "gracious," to saying "grace," to saying "thanks." We have only to notice how this is anchored at the heart of our worshiping life in the Church: in the Eucharist, the thanks-giving. Indeed, *one* of the central things we mean when we speak—if we do anymore—of a person as "gra-cious" is a person who is a thankful receiver: a thankful re-ceiver of all that comes to him. This is a hard lesson that we can try to learn from Paul. Thankfulness is the very heart of the Christian's life, for he knows that all that has worth is from God, that all that he has is from God; everything, in-cluding what he too hastily calls "good" or "bad." In short, the Christian gives thanks to God for all the sorts and condi-tions of his life. It is knowing how to say "Thanks."

Thanks, then, is the task laid on the receiver. *How* to say thanks is the strategy of stewardship. I conceive that that "strategy of how" is someone else's task because that is be-yond the scope of these remarks.

There is, however, more to be said about being grateful, more to be said about gratitude. *Gratis*, the word in grateful, in being thankful, is the word "free." Opposed, then, to *gratis* (free) is *ingratis*, ingratitude. This is very important for us. In the biblical understanding, *sin is fundamentally ingratitude* (Karl Barth). I will return to that point in conclusion, but for now I wish to say something more about freedom.

The Gospel always has to do with the freedom of man. Paul saw this clearly when he admonished the Galatian church: "For freedom Christ has set us free; stand fast therefore, and do not submit again to a yoke of slavery!" The freedom of the Christian can never properly be reduced to ideas of "liberation," for in our current use of "liberation," we are nearly always speaking of some specifically political or social liberation. *Not* all of the world's slaves are the poor, the deprived, the politically and socially bound. Whatever holds us—*and I'm addressing the ordinary Episcopalian*—is our master. Whatever holds us, whatever binds us, is our master.

If there is an ordinary Episcopalian, and I believe that there is such a thing, he is still wrestling, or ought to be wrestling, with the age-long "God and Mammon" problem. *Nothing enslaves us more than our money.* (Here, clearly, I am addressing the so-called "haves" directly, and not the so-called "have-nots," for it would be morally outrageous to address them in the tone of these remarks.) Our greatest need is to get free of our preoccupation with money. I simply do not believe that money is not a problem for the overwhelming majority of our American population, and hence of the majority of Episcopalians (or any other kind of American Christian for that matter). It is the one thing which most enslaves us. Money enslaves us by governing both our imaginations and our aspirations: How to get it if we don't have it, how to get more of it, or how to get rid of it if we have it. Stewardship has to do with getting free of what binds us, of getting free of our money. Stewardship is more than that, but it is *always* at least that.

"Best sellers" are very short-lived things. That it is a *best* seller, or that it *sells* better than other books is the principal measure of its worth. Recently, one of them has been Saul Bellow's novel, *Humboldt's Gift*. The hero, Charlie Citrine (actually he is no hero but only the principal character), is completely preoccupied with money. Citrine's main problem is what to do with the money he has, money he has earned and money that has come to him through a legacy of the unpublished literary works of his deceased poet friend, Von Humboldt Fleisher.

Charlie Citrine has succeeded in the world's way of success. He is a historian, author of important books, author of a

long-running and highly successful play. He has invested his
money, making and losing several small fortunes. He has
moved in the jet-set entourage of President Kennedy. He has
married well and the marriage has failed. He drives the most
elegant Mercedes, wears the best Italian leather shoes, is
modish in his dress. He flirts with other money-obsessed
people, for example small-time underworld figures. He
squanders money on things, on women, on fools, and on
hopeless but grand-seeming projects. His base is Chicago, a
city built on commerce and money. Bellow's novel catches
us—contemporary America—as we were—as we are: obsessed with money and what it will buy, obessed with money
and how to get rid of it, trying to get free of what chiefly binds
us. Charlie Citrine is massively unhappy. He is unfree.
Money is master. He is its slave.

All of this is the familiar idiom of countless preachers. That
it is familiar only makes it more terrifying since we are therefore allowed the beguilingly dubious luxury of dismissing it
as a cliché while we continue with our preoccupation and ob-
session with money. Simply put, one of the greatest spiritual
needs of contemporary Americans is that of getting free of
our money, for it is that—money—which chiefly binds us.
We have come, however, like the most submissive of slaves to
love our bonds.

In this instance to love our bonds is to love our death. I am
aware that the accusation of melodrama can be brought
against such a view as the one which I put forth here. That is
only a hedge. It is only a dodge. Anyone who has ever at-
tempted to confront himself, let alone another person, with
what he is doing with his money knows that we are capable
of endless deceptions, capable of manufacturing thousands of
excuses masquerading as reasons, for why we don't do
differently with what we have. What we have (or think we
have) has come to have us. We are possessed. It is possession
of all sorts from which Christ has come to set us free. "Why
will you, then, submit again to a yoke of slavery?" Because
it's easier to submit. God help us!

To be able to give, however, is a mark of freedom. In fact,
giving is freedom, since truly *to give* is to act without con-

straint or obligation. To pay wages, to meet obligations, is not—as we have seen—meaningfully or truly spoken of as freedom, though we may have freely entered a wage or contractual relationship. "Freely you have received. Freely give."

To be able to give is a mark of humanity, and the true mark of humanity (with capacity for giving, that is, with capacity for freedom) is seen in Jesus. "Jesus," someone has said, "is God's idea of what it is to be a human being." Again, we are dependent upon a gift for the very vision of "God's idea of what it is to be a human being." Jesus himself is a gift. "God so loved the world that he gave. . . ." Loving and giving and freedom are necessarily, for us, tied closely together.

Principally, so far I have tried to speak of the *positive* things about giving. About being grateful, I have said that it is a mark of freedom. There is, however, one other thing to be said, something to which I alluded previously: Fundamentally, all sin is ingratitude. That is a view of sin which is opposed to the more typical and common view of sin as some specific *negatively* valued act. It is too comfortable when we narrow our notion of sin to transgression of some law, or some norm. Such transgressions are serious and I do not wish to belittle them in importance. I am, however, dwelling on something else here.

Usually, pride is said to be—and properly—the most grievous sin. (It could be shown that sloth, envy, anger, lust, greed, and gluttony all flow from pride as from the principle of the so-called "seven deadly sins.") Pride is really ingratitude. The prideful person literally says "thanks" for nothing. The prideful person views himself as the source and origin of good things, and as the final criterion for judging what is good and what is bad. He himself is the imagined conferrer of worth. That is, for the prideful person, all things have whatever value they have because they derive from him or from his valuing of them. In short, "I am the determiner of the worth of things." "I am the center of the universe." Functionally and effectively, that is what pride is like.

The other side of pride is freedom, love, thankfulness, gratitude. The other side is that of the lover who is in constant acknowledgment that, whatever one's circumstances, *life is a gift*—from God. The lover acknowledges that the one appropriate response, as a Christian, is gratitude, is the gift of himself. That is, finally, the lover tenders back to God not only what he *has*, but what and who he *is*. He can tender it to God only by giving himself away for the life of the world.

J. C. Michael Allen

Mike lived up to his reputation as the bold, activist rector of historic St. Mark's in the Bowery when I first heard him keynote an MRI conference in Chicago in the early sixties. Arraying himself against those who profited from the intolerable status quo in the Bowery, Mike had spent time in jail after demonstrating for open housing, opened the church to playwrights, actors, poets, painters, filmmakers, and a creative new liturgy. After a stormy and fruitful ministry there, Mike took on the unenviable task of saving Berkeley Divinity School from financial collapse. He engineered an affiliation with Yale Divinity School that not only improved the Anglican presence on the campus of that great university but the quality of both divinity schools as well. His mission fulfilled, Mike accepted the call as Dean of Christ Cathedral, St. Louis, Missouri, returning to his real love, the urban ministry. Someone once defined stewardship as "the ordering of one's life so that the Gospel of Christ may be shared with all men and women." Mike, as much as anyone I know, has done that.

Money and Grace

WHEN I WAS A CHILD I dreamed of a new world, I dreamed of a world where nobody would ever be hurt or afraid or alone. I dreamed of a new world where my mother and father and all my friends and I would be happy and joyful for ever and ever.

And then I grew up. And I faced the hard reality of life and I gave up my dream of a new world—as most people give up their dreams. And I lived as the world told me to live. I did not like my grown-up life very much.

When I became a child again, when by God's grace I became his child and he became my father, and I joined his Church and became part of the body of Christ, I no longer dreamed of a new world; I lived in a new world.

Now I live in that new world whenever I gather with my brothers and sisters to hear the Lord's word, and break the Lord's bread, and sing the Lord's praises. I receive from the Lord's hand all I will ever need to live, and my brothers and sisters beside me receive all they will ever need. And I hear the Lord say to me that one day all the world will be like this and all his people will be gathered together in a world where no one will ever cry again or hurt again. Some day he will call all the world's people out of their tombs and into his life where they will live happily and joyfully for ever and ever.

I know this is true, and it is not a story or a myth, because I live it and because I know this: On the day the Lord Jesus died on the cross . . . "the veil of the temple was torn in two . . . and the rocks were split, and many bodies of the saints who had fallen asleep were raised, and coming out of the tombs after his resurrection they went into the holy city and appeared to many" (Matt. 27:51–53).

You and I stand in those open graves right now. We may walk if we wish. We may live in a new world, a new society, a society where men and women are free to live and love and work and play as one with their risen Lord. Or we may stand in our open graves and go nowhere, bound by chains that are broken, customs that have no hold, death that has lost its sting.

And the Church to which we belong, the body of Christ, is the risen body, the body that came down from the cross, that was buried in the tomb, and that came out anew and fresh from that tomb to proclaim to the world that death is overcome: henceforth the world will live by his life and love by his love.

You are a body of freedom, the very body that stands in the open grave ready to walk, or a body of death that denies freedom, pulls the grave in over its head, and dies the second death.

A master went away on a long trip. He left his possessions behind for his servants to use. To one servant he left five talents, and to another two, and to yet another one, each according to his ability. I am sure he told them to invest the money, to put it to work for his purposes. And what other purpose could there be but to care for his flocks, to feed his people, to enrich and beautify his lands.

The first servant, believing his master's purposes to be honorable, invested the money and gained more, and I am sure he spent more and enriched his master's estates. And so did the second. But the third believed his master to be a scoundrel and, in that belief, that his master would never share his money or use it for any good purpose, buried it all.

When the master returned he asked for an accounting and when the first servant told him he had invested the money, and how much he had gained for him, the master was overjoyed and said to him, "Well done, good and faithful servant; you have been faithful over little, I will set you over much: enter into the joy of your master." And when the second servant showed his master what he had done with the money, his master said the same to him. But when the third servant told the master what he believed to be true, "I knew you to be a hard man, reaping where you did not sow, and gathering where you did not winnow; so I was afraid and I went and hid your talent in the ground. Here you have what is yours." Then the master replied, "Don't be surprised then that I am what you believe me to be, a hard man." And he cast him into outer darkness, into the very darkness he had chosen for himself by rejecting his master's love (Matt. 25:14–30).

Certainly the graves are open, but you and I and all God's people choose for ourselves whether we shall walk out of our graves or make our open graves our home.

When the Old Testament tells the story of creation in all its richness, it tells us who we are as men and women. It says that we betray each other and we betray God. It says we have poisoned our own atmosphere, that we have turned the Garden of Eden into hell, and that we are outcasts on the face of the earth. All this the authors know and so do we. But they know something far more important about our world. And about us. They know that God made this world. They know he made it as a Garden of Eden, to be loved and enjoyed, to be lived in forever in peace, harmony, justice, and love. If it is no longer such a garden, it is because we chose it to be otherwise.

Genesis says that God made Adam and Eve to till the soil and tend the garden and enrich the whole earth. He who did this, who made the world and men and women, is therefore the creator. And the creator of everything is the Lord of everything, and the Lord of everything is master of everything.

God gave this world to us in trust. Nothing belongs to us. Possessions of the earth and of the mind, wealth in all its forms are gifts of God to be used to enrich creation, to enrich all life, plant life, animal life, human life, so that nature may sing the praises of its creator. Therefore, neither money nor any possession at all is to be hoarded. It is not to be accumulated mindlessly as if it could take the place of the loving hand of God. But money and all possessions are always to be used for the enrichment of God's world and everything and everybody in it.

To such a vision Paul called the early Church: To a world of unity and equality, where every man, woman, and child is equally precious and equally dear in the eyes of God. And the symbol he used, the means he used was money: a great collection of money that would state the unity of the Church, that would proclaim the grace of God.

The early Church was torn between the Jewish Christians in Jerusalem and the gentile Christians elsewhere. It was torn between Pharisaic Christians who lived passively in the fear of God, waiting for the Lord to transform the world; and revolutionary, would-be Christians who intended to unify all of Israel into one great attack force against the Romans. And there were countless more divisions, some great, some small.

Peter was leader of one group. Paul was leader of another. Everybody questioned the validity of each other's call, and the Church awaited then, as it does now, some great unifying act, some statement that we are all brothers and sisters in Christ, called to one purpose, called to one life despite all our divisions.

In the midst of all this tension and all this trouble, calamity hit the church in Jerusalem. Poor already, struggling for survival amidst the power of the Pharisees, the crops failed, and the church suffered. It suffered intensely, and men and women starved. Perhaps it was the curious and sometimes paradoxical will of God that this happened, that in the weakness and the hurt of his people, the power of his grace might be revealed. And the instrument of that grace was the gentile church, the church for which Paul spoke and which he led. Because Paul preached a collection to aid the church in Jerusalem, a collection that would proclaim once and for all the unity of all Christians, the possible unity of all God's people, and the grace of God.

In that one collection—and it was a literal collection, money, gold and silver, desperately needed to buy grain and oil, to feed the hungry in Jerusalem—Paul saw his chance to proclaim the glory of God through the way Christians care for each other. "For you know the grace of our Lord Jesus Christ, that though he was rich, yet for your sake he became poor, so that by his poverty you might become rich" (II Cor. 8:9). "I do not mean that others should be eased and you burdened, but that as a matter of equality your abundance at the present time should supply their want, so that their abundance may supply your want, that there may be equality" (II Cor. 8:13–15).

The few pennies the poor church of the gentiles amassed into a collection for the starving church of Jerusalem might bring the great reward of the sharing of the spiritual riches of Jesus Christ, the sharing of the treasure of Jerusalem with the new churches of the gentiles—that there might be equality before the Lord.

The new world is not like the old world. In the new world

brothers and sisters do not let each other starve. Brothers and sisters do not let each other die, but brothers and sisters reach out to each other, not alone because there is pain, not alone because there is suffering, though all this cannot be allowed to exist in God's world, and we are called each and every one of us to compassion.

We reach out to each other in love to proclaim the glory of God, to proclaim that this is the way the Lord chooses his world to be—that in his world and in his sight all people are equally precious, equally dear.

In his sight we are all one, though many. The collection meant that Christians all over the Eastern Mediterranean gave of their hard-earned substance to proclaim the faith, to proclaim that they knew what life and money and pos-sessions and wealth were for. And their message was deli-vered. They were heard in that ancient world of theirs. Lu-cian, a second-century Roman, writes: "The efficiency the Christians show whenever matters of community interest happen is unbelievable: they literally spare nothing. And so, because Peregrinus was in jail, money poured in from them; he picked up a very nice income this way. You see, for one thing, the poor devils have convinced themselves they're all going to be immortal and live for ever, which makes most of them take death lightly and voluntarily give themselves up to it."

Paul died for the sake of his cherished collection. Because it was on his trip to Jerusalem to present the collection that the ruling authorities there finally became enraged that all this money had been collected all over the known world, not to enrich the Temple enterprise, not to maintain the structure of religion in Jerusalem, but to feed the poor. And so Paul chal-lenged the sin of the world which forever uses money for its own ends, rather than using money to make a new world, to feed the poor, to heal the sick, to proclaim the unity of God's people, and the glory of God himself.

So we now stand in our open graves and have the choice. We can live in those graves surrounded by our possessions, which will surely outlive us. They will shine in the light, but give us none of the light. They will buy food, but will not themselves feed us. Gold and silver will last forever but will give us none of their immortality. Or we can give of our substance, not alone to be generous, not alone to find peace in ourselves and meaning in our lives. Though what greater meaning can any person find than to save life and relieve pain? But we give of ourselves to proclaim the Lord's will that we and all our brothers and sisters live in unity and peace, that all our possessions be used to glorify his holy name.

We are not asked to be sad-faced like the hypocrites. We are not asked to give up our money so that we may starve. We are only asked that we recognize the Lord as the one Lord of our lives, to recognize all possessions—and money as the sign of those possessions—as the gift of God to be shared for the good of all humanity. And we are asked to build in our own Church a society of mutual caring, mutual giving, mutual loving that proclaims to the world the grace and glory of our God.

"I appeal to you therefore, brothers and sisters, by the mercies of God, to present your bodies as a living sacrifice, holy and acceptable to God, which is your spiritual worship. Do not be conformed to this world but be transformed by the renewal of your mind, that you may prove [live out] what is the will of God, what is good and acceptable and perfect" (Romans 12:1–2).

PART TWO
Methodology

James L. Sanders

"In case you don't know where Selma is, it might help if you remembered that it's in walking distance of Montgomery," so says Jim Sanders when he opens his address at a Provincial Stewardship Workshop. His workshop teammate, Mike Allen, had one day spent several hours in the Selma jail, checking out that walk. In spite of— or because of—all that has gone before, Jim is the dynamic rector of St. Paul's Episcopal Church, a flourishing, racially integrated Selma parish. After opening his workshop session with prayer and Bible readings, he proceeds to tell his group that tithing to the Church changed his life, and that of his entire family, for the better. A very successful pipe salesman for a national company before entering the ministry, Jim now "sells" the Alabama Plan with the same flair, and with added sincere, religious fervor. The Church leadership in the state of Alabama must be doing something right, because the giving per communicant per year is the highest in the American Church. Jim and his associate consultants have shared their talents, not only with our provincial workshops but with individual diocesan groups from Long Island to Texas. There's no one who can do it better than Jim. I'm grateful for his talent but most especially for his friendship.

The Alabama Plan

THE QUESTION running through my mind as I sat in the parish hall of the Church of the Nativity in Huntsville, Alabama, in the fall of 1969 was: "What in the world is going to happen here in the next two days?" I had received the letter asking me to attend a stewardship workshop in order to be trained as a stewardship consultant, but the leaders had not briefed me as to my role in this particular weekend.

Standing around before the meeting began, I noticed that the group was made of laymen from the Nativity parish, a few diocesan staff members, and two or three other clergymen from other parishes in the surrounding area. (I was one of the "two or three clergymen from other parishes.") The setting was familiar: newsprint was hung, felt markers were evident, and of course the guy nearest these objects was the "well-trained," "deeply sensitive," "highly skilled" coordinator of our two-day meeting on stewardship. I was also aware that this meeting was going to be like other meetings in our diocese—open; that is, from the beginning we would have laid out for us what the participants could expect from the staff and what would be expected from us. I knew this because Alabama had a large percentage of clergy who were skilled in designing and conducting experiential education activities. What I did not know was how *experiential education* had anything to do with *stewardship.* In my way of thinking stewardship was the Every Member Canvass, meeting the budget—in short, raising money. The only *experience* I could relate to was a kind of sick feeling in my stomach when that time of the year rolled around when the parish had to be asked for more money. It looked to me as if I was in for two days of boredom and negative feelings. What I heard and experienced was one of the most important events of my life. I had a conversion experience which has made Christian stewardship real to me. That two-day conference was the beginning of a process which allowed me to re-think the meaning of *freedom in Christ* and the commitment necessary to that freedom.

It all began (at least for the Diocese of Alabama) following a diocesan council meeting in the spring of 1969. The idea of a diocesan stewardship education project was born in a conversation between the Rev. William A. Yon, program development coordinator for Alabama, and the Rt. Rev. Furman C. Stough, then diocesan missioner. These two staff members

had attended a council meeting where it had become apparent that the congregations would have to be asked to increase
their giving if the diocesan budget was going to be met. Mr.
Yon said the question was: "Will the congregations support
another increase?" The answer was: "We will have to go out
and sell them on the idea that the diocese needs more
money."

These two men, in their conversation, realized that
"whether or not a parish could give more money to the diocese depended ultimately on individuals increasing their giving to parishes." It was obvious that if the diocese was to receive more financial support, the parishes would first have to
increase communicant pledges. The task was clear: come up
with a process which would increase pledges at the grass
roots level. Incidentally, by having people in staff positions
who are skilled in coordinating programs, a diocese can really
aid parishes on the local level while increasing the effectiveness and effort on a diocesan level. This is the best way to get
away from the "we" (parish) and "they" (diocese) syndrome
which is so prevalent throughout our Church today, and start
a return to an early "Christian family" attitude.

It would be helpful at this point to refer to a report written
to the Stewardship Committee of the Diocese of Alabama
concerning the creative work done by Bishop Stough and Mr.
Yon. The pronoun "we" refers to the two then-staff members.

> The following is a description of the *process* which began to un-
> fold. It is a description of the *creation of a diocesan resource,* not
> another guide to running a snappy Every Member Canvass at the
> parish level.
>
> Based on our experience, we are convinced that it is a process
> that is replicable in any diocese or judicatory which:
>
> (a) has a team of persons who are skilled in designing and con-
>   ducting experimental education activities, and who are also
>   personally committed to proportionate giving as a pattern for
>   Christian stewardship;
>
> (b) is willing to assign sufficiently high priority to the project to
>   make available 30 to 40 days of staff or volunteer time during
>   the first year; and
>
> (c) seriously wants to provide help rather than apply pressure as a
>   way of increasing giving to the Church.

A number of documents which developed during this process are attached as appendices to this report. They are not included in the report itself because (a) they became very lengthy; (b) their function is indicated in the report itself; (c) there is nothing magic about any of them—any diocese needs to produce its own documentation; and (d) it is the *process* which is replicable, not the detailed step-by-step mechanics.

Initial Reflections

We knew that there were reliable ways of helping a congregation increase its level of giving. Bill Stough had had experience in using a professional stewardship organization in his parish—at a cost of several thousand dollars—and knew that it worked.

We wanted to create a resource that would cost a congregation something, but much less than several thousand dollars.

We knew of congregations that used outside professionals, showed dramatic increases in pledging (up to 100 percent), then experienced a decline in giving over the next several years.

We wanted to create a resource that would show a less dramatic initial increase, but would lead to continuing growth in succeeding years.

We knew that professional organizations typically sent in a consultant who stayed on the scene for up to six weeks.

Knowing that that was impractical in most situations without great expense, and not wanting to make a career of it ourselves, we wanted to create a resource that would be effective with as little as 3 to 8 days time from an outside consultant.

We knew that professional organizations developed a tight package and required that client parishes follow every jot and tittle of their instructions.

We were interested in developing a more flexible style that could shape itself to local conditions, and that would create self-reliance in parish leaders rather than dependence.

Assuming that the professionals had no magic, but only time and skill, we agreed to take the time and hoped to develop the skill to provide an effective resource for stewardship education in any parish which felt a genuine need for it.

Basic Elements

First, we isolated the basic elements of the professional services which we knew to be effective. They did not seem to be very complicated:

(1) an *outside* consultant
(2) to whom the congregation made a *commitment* (time and money)

(3) who helped local people develop a sound and workable *plan*
(4) and who provided *training* for those who would actually do
the work.

Pilot Projects

Next we had to see if we could put together something that
would work. We immediately thought of three congregations
which had indicated that they needed some help in the area of
stewardship, and which might be willing to try something new
with us. Before we could complete our thinking on this, a fourth
came on the scene, so we wrote: "A Proposal for Four Pilot Projects in Stewardship Education in the Diocese of Alabama—1969–
1970."

The proposal made it clear that we were trying to see if this
thing would work. Its goals were: (a) to increase the level of giving
in the four pilot congregations; (b) to develop models for stewardship education which could be used elsewhere; and (c) to begin
developing a team of persons who could offer this service to other
congregations.

Each congregation was asked to agree to a five-phase project,
including follow-up evaluation.

Partly to humor us, partly because they really did need help,
the four congregations agreed to engage in the project. Bill Stough
and I planned jointly, but split up the four to see if we could discover how much effect, if any, the personal style of the consultant
had on results. He worked with two congregations, I worked with
one, and we worked together with one.

Giving in the four congregations increased from 10 percent (in a
congregation which had experienced a severe communicant loss
the previous year) to 45 percent. Careful analyses were written
and distributed. As word spread two other congregations asked
for "emergency" help which we supplied in the winter and spring
of 1970.

The key was obviously the recruitment of a large number of
canvassers and their thorough training. We devised a two-session
training design, each session taking three hours. Session II had
provided some practice experiences in canvassing and dealt with
the mechanics of pledge cards, reporting, etc.

The Church of the Nativity in Huntsville, Alabama, was
one of the four pilot projects. As I have said, it was in this
meeting that I started looking at Christian stewardship seriously. I was given an opportunity to look at that phrase
which is repeated (and has been for at least four centuries) in
the Anglican Communion: "All things come of thee, O Lord,

and of thine own have we given thee." (I Chron. 29:14) I had
never really understood what I was repeating. "All things"
literally means the air I breathe, the food I eat, the ground I
walk on, the talent for making a living I so often refer to as my
skill, my energy, my personality. "All things"—that's a tremendous trust fund. At any rate, the words "and of thine
own have we given thee" throws a whole different light on
giving. I am not giving anything, I am merely returning a portion to God of that which was given me.

I was thirty-seven years old at the time of the conference. I
had been a layman in the Episcopal Church, had completed
seminary, and was serving a parish; and yet I had never given
any thought (other than making a token pledge) to returning
to God a proportion of what God gave to me. To be perfectly
honest, I had never considered "giving to the Church" as
returning to God. "OK," I said to myself, "but if I am going to
return a proportion to God, what might that look like?" The
question had no sooner run through my mind when I heard
these words, "Tithing is a gracious norm for the individual's
giving—a fractional commitment which symbolizes total
commitment." At the dropping of this little bombshell in our
meeting, hands started shooting up all over the place, but to
be perfectly frank I did not hear the questions being asked by
the laymen in the room. I had had too much Bible study in
seminary not to know the "bad news." *Tithing* meant ten percent! I was caught, confronted, challenged, and the only
thought I had was to find an exit from the room. Now I had
begun to understand how it was possible to apply experiential education activities to stewardship training, and the dis-
covery was making me more than a little uncomfortable.

When I returned home at the conclusion of the conference,
my wife and I sat down and looked at our pledge to God
through his Church. We found that the fifteen dollars a
month we pledged was not in proportion to the "all" we received from God. By the same token we knew we were going
to have to start where we were and work toward a goal of
tithing. The Alabama Plan makes it clear that it is designed for
the "Christians who wish to become tithers, but cannot do so
immediately." A person can begin where he or she is and
work toward the goal of tithing.

We started where we were and, surprisingly, made our goal a few years later. I certainly wish I could tell you that great things started happening to us once we began to tithe. Unfortunately that was not our experience. The car, along with the washing machine and dryer, continued to break down. Medical bills were just as large, as were those for food and clothing. All in all, that first year was tough, and not just in a material way. It affected our family life by putting a strain on our emotions. It's not easy to explain to your children that something cannot be done because Mom and Dad decided to tithe. But maybe that's what was meant when they said "Tithing is . . . a fractional commitment which symbolizes total commitment." It really is more than just money. But let me say, a freedom event occurred in our lives once we began to tithe, which continues to astound us to this day.

The freedom we found might best be described in the Kris Kristofferson song "Me and Bobbie McGee:" "Freedom's just another word for nothing left to lose." When we realize that "all things come of thee, O Lord, and of thine own have we given thee," we realize that everything is his, and that we have nothing without him. That realization frees us from our pride; and after all, what is more freeing than to lose one's pride in material things. If pride (hubris) is the source of all our sin, and I believe this to be true, in losing pride we are free for a whole new way of living.

What happened in my life after my first conference on stewardship makes it easy to be a consultant in the Stewardship Education Program we have in Alabama. This program owes its success to the fact that it has trained consultants who believe their work is scripturally, theologically, traditionally, and intellectually sound. With this statement as a backdrop, I believe an overview of our process would be in order. The Rev. Bill C. Caradine, diocesan coordinator for stewardship in Alabama describes the process in the following statement:

Initial Contact

Initial contacts are made in several ways. In the past the diocese has taken the initiative to offer this program to specific parishes. Decisions about which congregations will be invited are made sometimes based on known information about their financial situ-

ation, upon recommendation of the bishop or another member of
the stewardship consultant team, or in response to an inquiry.
Other parishes become involved (especially those outside the Diocese of Alabama), having heard about the program, either by directly contacting one of the consultants, or by contacting the
diocesan coordinator (until recently, the Rev. Bill Yon, diocesan
program planning coordinator). To date, no congregations have
been invited to participate in this program simply by random
choice.

Exploratory Meeting

After an initial contact has been made, and if there is continuing interest, an exploratory meeting is arranged between a
consultant and the rector and his vestry and/or stewardship
committee. The purpose of the meetings are: (1) to describe the
services being offered by the consultant, which are: (a) *Diagnosis.*
To work with the vestry or other local committee in developing an
accurate description of the stewardship situation as it presently
exists in the congregation. (b) *Planning.* To consult with the local
committee in developing an effective plan of action that will take
into account both the unique conditions of the local congregation
and the experience of other congregations which have been involved in similar efforts. (c) *Training.* To design and conduct a
training program for members of the congregation who will be
given an opportunity to volunteer their services as canvassers. (d)
Evaluation. To work with the local committee in developing an accurate description of the results of the project. (e) *Follow-up.* To
work with the local committee in projecting an effective plan of
action for succeeding years.

(2) To negotiate the expectations the consultant will have of
the particular parish. Some of the expectations to be negotiated
are: (a) That the rector be a tither, or that he be committed to the
principle of tithing as a goal and be systematically working toward
that goal. (b) That the leadership of the parish accept the principle
of proportional giving, with the tithe being a minimum standard
and goal for themselves, and that they be willing to commend this
principle to the rest of the congregation. (c) That the vestry accept
the concept of proportionate giving as a model for its own stewardship of the parishes' resources. (d) That the vestry commit itself to assuring that a personal call will be made into the home of
every communicant, including a call on the rector and his family.
(e) That the diocese will pay the expenses of an initial visit by a
consultant to a parish, and that the parish would then pay an
agreed-upon amount for any further services of the consultant.
(Within the diocese fees are usually $50.00 per day plus travel and
lodging.)

This is a crucial step in the program since the vestry can, by its attitude, seriously affect the success or failure of a stewardship program.

The behavior of a consultant is critical at this point. If his criteria for personal success is that the vestry buy his package, he is in for trouble. If he is flexible, and quite willing to say no to the vestry, or to have the vestry say no to him, he is generally on pretty safe ground.

If an agreement is reached between a consultant and vestry, the agreement should be reduced to a written instrument. The instrument would set out precisely all areas of agreement.

When an agreement is reached the following action steps and target dates will usually be established:

(1)   The consultant will begin to gather data, and will prepare a thorough analysis of the present stewardship situation.

(2)   A decision will be made as to how many co-chairmen and captains will be needed, and it is decided who will recruit them, and when they will be recruited.

(3)   A date is set for the next visit of the consultant for the purpose of planning the stewardship program, including a specific time line of target dates, and for training the rector, chairmen, and captains. This usually requires two days of the consultant's time.

A time line usually looks something like this:

A. After the planning session and training session for chairmen and captains, a third visit by the consultant is scheduled— usually two to three weeks later. During this period of time, the following things happen:

(a) Canvass calls are made into the homes of the rector, chairmen, and captains, and they make their pledges. The way this usually works is that the rector and chairmen call on one another in a round robin process, and the chairmen call on the captains.

(b) The captains are responsible for recruiting consultant/ canvassers for their teams. The goal for the number of consultant/canvassers is one for every four families in the congregation. (This is usually a difficult task, and if not accomplished, can endanger the entire program.)

B. The consultant returns for training session #1 for consultant/canvassers. (At least two sessions being offered.) After training session #1, and before the consultant returns for training session #2 (usually two weeks), the following is to happen:

(a) Captains are to make calls into the homes of the consultant/canvassers on their teams to receive their pledges.

(b) Publicity campaign is intensified.

The above are important steps for at least three reasons: (1) By this time at least ¼ of the congregation will have been canvassed. (2) Usually the most significant increases in giving come from the canvass staff and their responses usually are a positive motivation to complete the task. (3) It becomes obvious that the leadership of the stewardship program will not ask others to do something that they have not already done.

C. Consultant returns for training session #2. Training session #2 is primarily concerned with the mechanics of calling. Two sessions are usually required. The actual canvass date should follow by at least one week, allowing for the following:

   (a) Each consultant/canvasser to send a postcard to the families that he will call on, telling them who will call, for what purpose, and the approximate hour that he will arrive. This has proven to be important for at least the following reasons: (1) It places the responsibility on the family to be called on to be at home to graciously receive the caller; or, if unavoidably away on the day of the canvass, to set another date for the visit; or, to say to the church's representative, "I don't want you to call." (2) It lessens the sense of being a door-to-door salesman on the part of the consultant/ canvasser. (3) Sets an agenda for the consultant/canvasser thereby encouraging him to complete his task in an orderly manner.

D. The consultant may or may not be present on the day of the actual canvass. At any rate, any canvass that is well organized can be completed in two to three hours—except for legitimate call-backs. No canvass should linger more than one week beyond canvass day.

E. Date for an evaluation can be mailed to a consultant and he can complete the evaluation in his office thus reducing time and travel involvement of the consultant, and cost to the parish.

F. Follow-up—A congregation might decide to use the services of a consultant to plan a continuing canvass program.

It is fair to assume that Mr. Caradine's description of this process will raise such questions in the reader's mind as:

1. How can the agreement between consultant and vestry be reached?
2. How much consultant time will be required?
3. What can be expected from a training session?
4. How is the canvass evaluated?
5. What can the parish expect from the follow-up?

The Alabama Plan provides instruments designed to produce answers to these questions. It should also be noted that the initial contact comes as an invitation and not as a directive from the front office. Bill Yon says the "You have been chosen as one of many" approach is more successful than the "We have noticed you are having trouble with stewardship, so we want to change that for you." The first is infinitely easier for a vestry to hear. Therefore, the first paragraph of Bill Caradine's statement (Initial Contact) should be taken in its entirety and studied carefully by the diocesan staff.

The statement that, "I (or we) do not have a plan for stewardship in our lives," is a false statement. Everyone has a plan for stewardship. That plan might range from, "I (we) give what's left over to God—if there is anything," all the way to "I (we) have a need to return to God a proportion of that which he has provided me (us) in order that his work might be done in this world." In Alabama, the stewardship committee has become more and more aware that a theological statement of stewardship worked through by the vestry and the diocesan council is an important step in purposeful and successful stewardship.

There are other steps, or building blocks, as Bill Caradine points out. I will list these by title even though they need further explanation:

1. Thorough Plan of Action
2. Theological Purpose
3. Adequate and Committed Staff
4. A Thorough Staff-Training Program
5. A Thorough and Purposeful Publicity and Educational Program

All of these require the assistance of a consultant.

The Diocese of Alabama has been conducting stewardship education training inside and outside Alabama for seven years. We started with the creative work of two men and have expanded our program. We have been careful to collect and collate extensive data as we have moved through the process, and know now that we have a workable plan for effectively working in the area of Christian stewardship. A synopsis of what a parish might expect if the Alabama Plan is used has been written by our stewardship coordinator. He was able to make this statement after many hours of pouring through results of our efforts, and many hours of staff input by the consultants. I would like to offer his statement as a fair, even though incomplete, synopsis of expectations.

A Synopsis of What A Congregation Might Expect to Have Happen When They Involve Themselves in the Diocesan Stewardship Education Program

This synopsis really addresses itself to two questions. First, what might a congregation expect to have happen as they involve themselves in the process of a stewardship education program? Second, what final results might a congregation expect, having involved themselves in a stewardship education program?

Question 1.   A congregation can expect its leaders to carefully, and prayerfully, examine and proclaim their individual principles of Christian stewardship. A congregation can also expect its leaders to carefully, and prayerfully, examine and proclaim the corporate principles of Christian stewardship of the congregation itself.

A congregation can expect to involve itself in a systematic methodology which proclaims the needs of the congregation, which allows every member the opportunity to reflect on their theology of Christian giving, and which assures that *every member* is asked to declare their intention to give a portion of their material resources for the Christian work of their congregation.

Each person who actively works in the stewardship program can expect to have the opportunity to articulate their personal beliefs about Christian giving, and to have their beliefs reinforced or changed as a result of their participation. This opportunity is provided during the training of stewardship program workers.

Question 2.   The results that a congregation might expect from having involved itself in the process of the Diocesan Stewardship Education Program are really of two kinds. First, there are the tangible results which can easily be tabulated and evaluated. The second kind of results are less tangible and much more difficult to tabulate and evaluate.

The history of the Diocesan Stewardship Program assures us that any congregation which conscientiously involves itself in the process can expect an increase in the number of its pledges, and an increase in the amount of its pledged income—usually a substantial increase. This is true, in part, because the process of the program itself requires that *every* member of the congregation be asked, personally, to make a pledge using the principle of proportionate giving as the basis for their action.

The Diocesan Stewardship Education Program does have an unresolved weakness. That weakness being that those who actively participate in the program are more deeply affected, and are usually more creatively responsive to the program than those who are later called on in their homes.

There are numerous less tangible results that congregations can expect from their involvement in the process of the stewardship program. Among those results are the following:

1. Almost without exception, a congregation involved in the stewardship program deals effectively with some nagging entry problems into the lifestyle of the congregation. This seems to happen for at least two reasons. First, the process itself tends to spotlight the needs of the congregation and allows a person to identify for himself/herself a place in the meeting of the congregation's needs. Second, the process itself allows for some significant interpersonal encounter, and for the affirming of the individuality within the church family.

2. Involvement in the process almost always gives birth to some new and effective leaders within a congregation.

3. Involvement in the process almost always transfers over to an increased participation in the worship life of the congregation.

4. Involvement in the process almost always creates motivation, and demands, to pursue other goals of the congregation.

5. Involvement in the process almost always provides a congregation with a success experience.

It is my personal bias that the less tangible, less measurable benefits that might accrue to a congregation are of greater value than the more obvious and measurable benefits.

There has accumulated a substantial bank of hard data—and a six-year history—which validates the assertions made in this synopsis. However, it needs to be said that participation in the stewardship program places some strenuous demands on a congregation. If the program is to succeed, a congregation must provide strong, open, committed leadership. A congregation must be able to assure that at least ¼ of its membership will actively participate in the process. A congregation must be willing to "buy into" a tested methodology, and pursue the process doggedly to its completion. A SUCCESSFUL PROGRAM REQUIRES VERY HARD WORK FROM A SUBSTANTIAL NUMBER OF PEOPLE.

I have tried in this chapter to give the reader a concise explanation of the Alabama Plan. At the same time I would like to emphasize that ours is only one approach to Christian stewardship. You have, in this book, other solid and successful approaches to consider. I believe our plan to be better only because it is the best way we have found to realize the promise of our Lord that, as good stewards, we will more fully participate in the "abundant life." My experience has been that a large percentage of Christians feel guilty about the way they share their material gifts. In attempts to keep from intruding into a person's money affairs, the Episcopal Church (especially the clergy) has kept a low profile. It is my opinion that the term "low profile" when used to describe our past stewardship responsibility would better be translated "cop-out." The Episcopal Church is renowned for its low per capita "giving" (a well-known statistical fact). This has not only crippled our effort "to do good, and to distribute" (Heb. 13:16) as a community of believers, but it has kept individuals in bondage, and thus hindered their experience of the freedom a Christian is offered. As ordained bishops, priests and deacons, and as lay ministers of the Gospel, we have as our responsibility the education of every man, woman, and child about the freedom found in Christian stewardship. If you and I do not provide this education—who will?

George F. Regas

When we met George Regas at our Provincial Stewardship Workshop in Dallas in 1974, his reputation as a powerful and committed Christian leader had preceded him. I've never heard a more dynamic presentation in my life in the Church! Had George chosen a profession in the theater, he would have been an outstanding success. It is no wonder he raises more money each year "from the living" than any other parish priest in the Episcopal Church. The biennial Goal Budget for All Saints, Pasadena, for 1977–1978 is $1,600,000! George has shared his extraordinary stewardship talents with groups all across the country, always receiving an incredible response. It is interesting that from a Greek Orthodox heritage, he chaired the Policy Board of the National Coalition for Women's Ordination to the Priesthood and the Episcopacy, and, as a deputy, took a leadership role in that debate at the General Convention in Minnesota. Without reservation, I commend George's stewardship methods to you.

Six Steps to Stewardship Development

I'VE NEVER FOUND the task of funding the Church's mission an easy one. Although we've had some success at All Saints Church, I somehow always feel we are on our last leg. I wonder if we'll make it. Will we end up the year in the red?

Then when I hear myself and others saying the Church is on its last leg, I think: But the Christian Church has always been on its last leg! Things have always been precarious! It's not an easy task these days to fund the mission of the Church, nor is it easy to be a parish priest in these uncertain times.

I heard a story the other day of a clergyman who became rector of a very difficult but important parish. He asked his predecessor if he'd sit down and spend the day with him going over all of the problems he would face, and share his advice on dealing with many of the obstreperous people of the parish. He was just asking for some insight into what that church was like. He hoped to avoid the fate of his predecessor in being gently removed from his position. At first, he refused to help. "No, I can't do that. It's your job. You've got to do it as best you can, so go to the work and God bless you." The new man persisted: "I want to get from you some idea about what's going on here and how I can do the job successfully." The former rector finally agreed to help. "I'll prepare for you two envelopes so that when times get hard you can open those envelopes and perhaps find some direction." So he gave the new rector two envelopes marked Number 1 and Number 2, and the rector put them away in a desk and promptly forgot about them.

About three years later things were really getting to be difficult. He remembered those envelopes and opened the first one. All it said was: "If you've reached the end of your rope, tie a knot and hang on." He certainly didn't find that advice very helpful! But he did hang on for a few more years. Finally, in another desperate moment, he remembered the second envelope. When the opened envelope Number 2, all it said was: "Prepare two envelopes." Well, some of us know what that means, don't we?

Let me tell you something about All Saints Church, Pasadena, so you will have a context in which to place my comments.

1. We have an annual budget of $525,000. We have no endowment; it is all from the living.

2. There is the staff of the rector, four clergy assistants, and eight other professional assistants.
3. The congregation consists of 2,700 communicants, 4,000 baptized people. It is a large and very diversified group.
4. Our whole life and ministry affirms pluralism and diversity— racially, economically, politically, and theologically. We have emphases on spiritual nurture and personal growth as well as a commitment to the poor and oppressed—a ministry of social activism.
5. I've been the rector for nine years. During the first three years the budget went from $200,000 to $380,000. Then for three years we stayed even. Ashley Hale came on the scene in 1973 as a stewardship consultant to the Diocese of Los Angeles and ten pilot parishes of which All Saints Church was one. In 1974 we went from $380,000 to $500,000; the 1969 average pledge was $6.00 per week; the 1974 average pledge was $12.50 per week.
6. All Saints Church has had considerable success with its fund raising; still our goals and aspirations far outreach the financial resources which are committed to us. We continue to struggle and stretch.

Winston Churchill was once given a plaque by the women's temperance union—if you can imagine that—and as the chairwoman gave Sir Winston this plaque she said, pointing to an imaginary line on the wall, "Sir Winston, do you realize that if we poured into this room all the brandy that you have consumed in your lifetime the mark would reach to about here?" Churchill, looking at the imaginary line on the wall and then at the ceiling, said, "So much to be done and so little time to do it."

Most of us feel that way, no matter where we stand in the development of stewardship. If you are sensitive at all to what God is calling us to do, you realize that your time is so short and the demands are so great.

I believe there are six principles to effective fund raising— or perhaps it's better to say six fundamental principles—the violation of which makes you swim up stream. Each parish finds its own path to a higher permanent level of giving. I would make no pretense that I can predesign your success. It is true that no two people swing a golf club exactly alike, but those who swing effectively can be observed to have certain aspects of their swing in common. So it is, in my opinion, with effective fund raising.

I
You Must Have a Plan

In the secular field it is clearly established that the organizations which are most successful in securing voluntary financial support are invariably well-planned organizations. They have well-thought-through goals and objectives, and a fair idea of how they are going to achieve these goals. They have good leadership who can clearly articulate a case.

Stewardship is a tool for congregational development—an incredible means of revitalization of people, of community, of mission. Giving a congregation a say in developing their own plan of action is a key to renewal and enrichment of lay participation.

A parish should articulate its purpose—what it wants to accomplish. This is where we want this church to be in two or three years, and this is what it all costs. Two years ago we produced such a plan for All Saints Church around three questions: What must we do? What should we do? What would we like to do? These questions were applied to three areas of concern under which the total ministry of the parish falls: services to the community, diocese, and world; services to our members; services to our buildings and grounds. We worked on it for four months involving open hearings, research and discussion, community input, and dinner parties of 800–900 people. We knew one thing: Those whose support of this plan was crucial to its achievement must be heavily involved in the planning process. It must be their plan. No one reacts enthusiastically to someone else's plan, so involvement is critical. Apathy is working on someone else's agenda.

A parish whose plan is the rector's plan can relax. The rector is now fully responsible for accomplishing the parish objectives. A plan created and owned by the congregation is absolutely essential to effective fund raising.

II
High Goals

Little plans generate little gifts.

In the secular field money is flowing to large, daring, well-thought-out goals. The size of the gift tends to be commensurate with the size of the vision. I once heard a wealthy IBM executive say that he would never give money to a college that didn't have stupendous dreams. The Church needs large goals—large enough really to matter. Don't let anyone in the parish cut back your dreams. Most treasurers are always moaning, "We can't raise that much!" And they are right. Negative predictions are self-confirming.

Emerson said once with respect to an individual's planning of his life: "Be careful lest you set your goals too low." We've got to think big if miracles are to happen. The Christian faith was never so desperately needed. "Religion divorced from civilization goes to seed. Civilization divorced from religion goes to hell."

I don't think it is possible to do the kind of job the world so desperately needs from the Church today if we are timid about our aspirations. I simply cannot believe it when I read that some churches indicate to their members that they hope to raise their budget from $100,000 to $102,400 for the coming year. The Church is not experiencing easy times, and surely we ought to have an enormous vision of what the Church might do. That vision we then share with our people and challenge them to support it.

When All Saints Church finished its plan, the first phase was a two year goal $1.6 million—$800,000 per year or double the previous year's budget. No one sneered at that ambitious goal. The senior warden telephoned one parishioner, the

highest pledger in the parish, and asked if she would consider pledging $25,000 a year for two years. We needed that
kind of commitment to meet our goal. She wanted to discuss
her commitment with her attorney and accountant, and then
tell us her decision. When she called back the senior warden,
she said: "Yes, she would give $35,000 a year for two years."
She had misunderstood the amount. And, obviously, he had
asked too little.

Our goal was $800,000 and we got $500,000. One thing I am
absolutely sure of—you can't raise $300,000 if your goal is
$100,000. Instantly achieved goals aren't worth much.
Parishes who say they made their goals easily will never
really know what they *could* have raised. How do you know
how high you can jump if you can never kick off the bar?

Remember the words of Shaw: "Some people see things as
they are and say why. I dream things that never were and say
why not?" That is the kind of spirit within a parish that leads
to effective fund raising. With high goals and dreams, you
will enlist the best people available in your congregation for
the stewardship task. You hold up a dream, then take the
pledges, which are promissory notes that we commit ourselves to this task God has laid on us, and do as much of the
plan as you can then afford from pledges received.

III
Seek the Giver Not the Gift

Again we look to the secular field. Peter Drucker, the high
priest of management theory, makes a profound distinction
between making sales and making customers. Industry that
ignores that maxim is in trouble. So it is with the Church as
well. To seek the gift and not the giver is a very un-Christian
act. "Just give us your money and be quiet!"ᵗ is no way to do
the job of stewardship.

The best established truth in fund raising is that the extent
to which the donor is intrinsically involved in the organiza-

tion or the cause is the largest factor determining the degree of his commitment and generosity, or the priority that the Church will receive upon his time, attention, and money.

Be careful about those people who retreat to the periphery of Church membership! They stay on the rolls but make only token gifts and give only token support of any kind. Watch out for the token givers—whatever they are and whoever they are. I am especially fearful of vestry people who are token givers—those making $20,000 a year and giving $200 a year to the Church. They make me uneasy, for I don't trust their judgment about the task of the Church. They are a depressant on the dreams. They keep the whole Church on the defensive and they take an opposition view to everything progressive. I've never known anyone who really dared to think of great goals for the Christian enterprise and commit the Church to them who was a token giver. I've never known a token giver who would respond to a congregational program designed to radically increase stewardship understanding and performance.

The most vicious tactic of the token giver is to delay a decision or action that moves the Church forward. If we really mean business about raising money to do the job of the kingdom, then you'd better have around you those people whose giving reflects their commitment to that task.

Love that token giver and encourage his participation in the life and worship of the parish, but for Christ's sake—yes, for Christ's sake—keep him out of the vestry and key leadership positions in the parish if you can!

I am conscious that it isn't easy to be a good giver, especially when the pressures of inflation and economic insecurities plague us constantly. Yet a standard of living without a commensurate standard of giving demoralizes and corrupts us. Giving is important, even in hard times, because God has so constructed the universe and human life that those who give are alive.

The Church has to help a person come to that. You're not born a good giver; you learn it. The Christian community must help a person to become generous. How? By changing his life, by changing her priorities. That is some task, but that

is the task of the Church—doing something with the giver
and thereby enriching the gift.

IV
The Church Must Give Away Money

If the Church itself is not a giver, it will never inspire generosity from its members. If the Church itself is selfish with its resources and self-indulgent, it will then thwart generosity. A
static cannot create a dynamic!

All Saints Church in Pasadena hopes to reach a goal of
spending fifty percent in outreach and fifty percent on services to our members. In 1976 we are at thirty-five percent.
American Protestant Churches give about sixteen percent of
their income to those things that are not services to themselves, and most of the sixteen percent is simply their fair
share in denominational dues.

A rabbi, who is a close friend, says his synagogue has a
sliding scale of dues they charge their members for its operating budget. They don't use the word "giving" to describe
synagogue operations. They start using the word "giving"
when the temple is giving money away—from which the
donor gets no discernible direct benefits. Life is for giving
away: that is a radical assertion, no matter how often we've
heard it.

The main theme of the Bible is concerned with God's lavish
love for his people and God's concern for the well-being of
every person. No wonder Jesus ranked last the cozy and comfortable!

The Church must give too! The Church must communicate
its deep concern for all people as that concern is reflected in
its budget if it is to have integrity to its life and mission. The
Church must challenge the nation to give. Our wealth is un-
precedented; yet look at the poverty, lack of health care, in-
adequacies of education, enormous social needs of our urban

centers. There is unconscionable poverty in America. The Church must proclaim that we are bound together in a unity. Everyone is precious. No one should enjoy anything until everyone has the basics of life. A thousand people across this globe will die in the next hour from starvation and malnutrition.

The Church has a task. It is my conviction—it might not be yours—that the Church has a task to confront radically the institutions and structures of our nations to use the resources we have—and they are enormous resources—for the healing of life. If that is so, the Church has no integrity in that confrontation if it does not use its own resources for healing. There is no integrity to our challenge to the nation if we use only sixteen percent of our resources on outreach with most of that going to the diocese.

If our ministry doesn't reach out daringly to the poor, the hungry, the oppressed, the victims of war and injustice in an effort to create a new world, then something very important in the motivation of personal giving through the Church is lost. The Church proclaims this in many ways; one is through its budget.

Money talks! Oh the incredible power of a dollar! It can do so much to heal and redeem! When people see it can heal and give hope for a new life and a new world, they will gladly take a collection for those in need at Jerusalem—as did the early Church.

V

Organization to Do the Task

There is little integrity in high goals if we walk away and do not provide the means of implementation. Lots of people love working on goals and nothing else. There is something spiritually debilitating about that. To keep getting a glimpse of challenging goals and feeling urged to do something good in the world without translating that into action undermines character.

Over the last decade, American giving to all philanthropic causes has more than doubled—from 9.5 billion to 22 billion. Yet the rate of increased giving to churches is half the rate of increase to secular organizations and causes. As a percentage of American philanthropy over the last decade, religion has declined from 60 percent to 40 percent. That is a tragedy! We in the Christian Church should use the finest possible techniques for fund raising to support and sustain the most vital and essential institution in society. Make certain you utilize the secular skills available to you which are congruent with the Christian mission.

A central tenet of the Judaeo-Christian tradition is the preciousness and uniqueness of every individual. Yet most Every Member Canvasses treat everyone alike. Secular fund raisers know better and so should the Church. Also each parish is different and must be treated so.

So what we've done at All Saints Church is to develop three divisions: A, B, and C. Division A represents about one percent of the pledging families who have substantial financial means. We go to them first and set a high standard of giving. We recognize that influence always flows down; it seldom flows up. We spend much time with the vestry discussing very candidly their pledging. Afterwards we go to Division B, which is the rest of the pledging families. We share with these pledgers the high standard of giving set by the Division A people. This is a strong dynamic in our campaign. Divisions A and B are the pledging members of the parish and they receive the major energy of the campaign. When this aspect of our fund raising efforts is completed, we move on to Division C, which are the nonpledgers and the new people.

All giving is in a triangle, always, no matter what the parish is like. At the top are the large gifts. Ten percent of the people always give 35–40 percent of a parish's income. It is simply an illusion to think that you raise more money by broadening the bottom of that base. That is false. The professional fund raisers know that the way to raise more money is to lift the apex of that triangle. You don't set out to broaden the base but to raise the size of the gifts of the top giving families. High pace-setting pledges help to energize the entire campaign.

We are now on a two-year pledge which enables us to avoid three of the liabilities of an annual canvass. First, it avoids seeing the task of merely renewing the pledge which has expired, and it allows the caller to discuss stewardship and proportionate giving, challenging the family to substantially higher levels of giving.

Second, the annual canvass tends to correlate the parish budget with the pledge, so people are giving toward budget requirements of the Church rather than for the aspirations of the Church. They are giving for the needs of the institution rather than their own needs for integrity and wholeness.

Third, a two-year pledge gives you time really to go to work on the continuing stewardship enterprise. It allows you time to have an ongoing program in which you go back to those who are underpledging, pursue the nonpledgers and new people, develop deeper stewardship education, revise your goals for the parish, and monitor the pledge payments so that pledgers keep current and feel good about their financial commitment. Only when we went for a two-year pledge at All Saints Church, were we able to establish a significant stewardship development program.

VI

Personal Witness

Stewardship is the concept that all we have is from God—nothing is ours. We are only trustees—stewards over these great resources of life and energy and creativity. As faithful stewards, we use what God has given us to create a world of beauty and justice and peace, a world of health and plenty for all people, a world God wills us to shape as co-creators. Fund raising, on the other hand, is securing money to sustain this vital ministry of the new creation.

Many think that good stewardship teaching makes fund

raising unnecessary. If stewardship gets through to a person, some contend, he will give at a high level and all the Church's problems will be solved. If a person loves Jesus, all the Church's problems are over! It doesn't work that way, I assure you! If you substitute stewardship education for fund raising, you will invariably be underfinanced. Churches that avoid fund raising are strongholds for token giving. Stewardship education without fund raising is as incomplete as fund raising without stewardship. We should avoid exclusive extremes—only to teach or only to raise funds.

The best way to do both stewardship and fund raising is through a personal witness in the home. With candor a layperson shares what's happened to him or her: "This is what I'm giving; this is why I am giving it; this is what it has meant to my life." And, "These are the goals and aspirations that we have in our parish to do God's work. Will you try giving, yourself? Will you try giving at this level? Will you consider being one of four or five people in this church who are going to be giving fifty dollars a week?" The suggested asking used in the home call is a guess geared to a minimum pledge of one dollar per week for every thousand dollars of annual gross income. That kind of sharing intimately and candidly, yet gently, of where we are and what we believe, and then asking somebody to join us in this vital ministry, is the best way to combine stewardship and fund raising.

It is exciting to see what happens when people are willing to do that. It is a very invigorating thing to make that kind of witness. Without any arrogance a caller simply shares what he or she is in giving. Enormous liberation has come to our church with this kind of gracious candor. You know, there was a time when you would put a pledge in an envelope and seal it and put it under the table where nobody could ever see what was happening. Everything was secret. Nobody was to know what anybody was giving. Only God. Well, you pay a heavy price for that kind of secrecy.

We have brought a candor to our church which is absolutely refreshing. The vestry talks openly about income and about the percentage of income the pledge represents. They talk about where they are in their giving and where they hope to go—and why. The personal witness is crucially important, for it combines stewardship and fund raising by asking a person to join you at a certain level of pledging.

Let me just summarize what I have shared with you about the deepest things that I have in my heart on stewardship.

1. Have a plan.
2. Have big goals.
3. Seek the giver and not just the gift.
4. Create a church that has a sense of its own need to give its resources away for the healing of the world.
5. Develop the organization, the skills, and the tools to do the job and to do it adequately.
6. Then make a personal witness.

VII

Conclusion

All effective fund raising is at its heart a response to the incredible and lavish love of God. St. Paul says: "With your eyes wide open to the mercies of God, I beg you to present your bodies a living sacrifice, acceptable unto God."

During the Second World War, when the universities of England were plagued by skepticism and apathy, the late Archbishop William Temple led a mission to the University of Oxford. It was no modern, high-powered, highly financed evangelistic campaign, but in the words of one observer: "It stopped the rot in the Christian life of Oxford." On the last night of the mission, in St. Mary's Church, the crowded congregation of undergraduates was singing lustily the words of Isaac Watt's hymn, "When I survey the wondrous cross where the young Prince of Glory died." Dr. Temple stopped the singing before the last verse and said: "I want you to read over this verse before you sing it. They are tremendous words. If you don't mean them at all, keep silent. If you mean them even a little, and want them to mean more, sing them very softly." There was a hushed silence while every eye was fastened on the hymnal, and then the words were sung in a whisper:

Were the whole realm of nature mine,
That were an offering far too small,
Love so amazing, so divine,
Demands my soul, my life, my all

Do we mean it when we sing it or do we commit mass perjury? When we mean it, that is stewardship. When we translate it into the flesh and blood of dollars for the work of the kingdom, that is fund raising. Both are essential to the effectiveness of the Gospel.

W. Ebert Hobbs

The fact that Canon Ebert Hobbs is the only person who has made all nine provincial stewardship workshops attests to his personal commitment. From a background in the Anglican Church of Canada, Ebert has had many years of first-hand experience in stewardship and development as commissioner of the Diocese of Nova Scotia, executive director of the Department of Church Renewal with the National Council of Churches, and in his present position in Ohio as executive assistant to Bishop John Burt. It is worthy of note that in the past five years the Diocese of Ohio has overpaid its apportionment to the General Church Program by over $400,000. Ebert is the author of The Covenant Plan *and* A Guide For Visitors, *superior* Every Member Canvass *booklets, and has made them available to the Church through The Seabury Press. On the Advisory Committee for the Office of Development, Ebert has been a capable, innovative advisor. He was tapped by the Presiding Bishop as vice-chairman of an Executive Council committee to explore the possibilities of a national fund campaign. If you want to succeed in the matter of stewardship, pay attention to Ebert. You can't be a better steward of your time.*

The Covenant Plan

FAR TOO OFTEN the basis of our stewardship activity in a parish or diocese is that of a vestry accepting the reality of a financial problem and making a decision to find a person and a method to raise some money. It is a surface and pragmat⸵⸴ kind of experience and decision which we must internalize in some way if we are to be convincing in our presentations.

In my present position as executive assistant to the Bishop of Ohio the first priority on my time is to be the bishop's executive assistant; the second priority is my role as planning officer; and the third is the work of stewardship officer. The job description is such that I spend ten to fifteen percent of my time on stewardship teaching and Every Member Canvass training. What I have to say should be understood as the way one diocese approached a diocesan EMC program need with very limited staff time.

The stewardship program in the Diocese of Ohio had been carried on by the communications officer who distributed EMC materials and occasionally brought in experienced stewardship persons to conduct day-long workshops. This had gone on for a number of years, but by 1969 the workshops had lost their effectiveness and, for many persons, stewardship—particularly the Every Member Canvass approach—had lost its punch. Parish leaders had gone through the process of being stimulated by speakers only to find when they went home that they could not apply all that stimulation and those good ideas to their home parishes. They became very frustrated. When I arrived in the diocese they wanted help in getting the stewardship job done—not just inspiring speeches but practical help.

In this situation, it seemed apparent that three things needed to be done if the stewardship program was to get off the ground. The first was to have someone who was well trained in stewardship work and could develop trust among the clergy and the leading laity to head up a new diocesan push in stewardship training and programming. We would also have to offer the congregations help which they could perceive as being helpful, and we would have to develop a support system for the EMC parish leaders.

Those of us who were charged with leading the program in the diocese did have some things going for us. Many of the clergy and leading laity wanted help, and they said so. The bishop was supportive, and said so. And the diocese was ready for a change. These ingredients of expressed need, diocesan support, competent leadership and readiness are particularly helpful in launching a diocesan stewardship program. It is much like a visitor going to a house to make a call. If he is not committed himself, he transmits that lack of commitment to the people he is calling on, with the result that their response is more apathetic than if the visitor had been enthusiastic about his mission. Uncommitted people do not tell a very convincing or challenging story.

The process of parish involvement in Ohio started with a series of regional meetings in the month of June. The bishop wrote to all the clergy, inviting them and their designated lay leaders to join him at any one of these meetings. At these meetings Bishop Burt, who attended all of them, spoke of his own desire to have stewardship taken seriously by all parishes, his own understanding of what stewardship means, and his commitment to practicing proportionate giving in his life. He introduced me as the man he had chosen to give diocesan leadership in this field. I followed his presentation with an address offering my theology of stewardship and the kind of help we could offer to congregations. We proposed a training program for the fall, and promised to follow up these June meetings with more information on the training aids and a schedule of the training meetings.

Over the summer we wrote a manual for the guidance of parochial EMC committees and set up two series of regional training meetings for the fall. These were dinner meetings, the cost of which was partially underwritten by diocesan funds. There were two meetings in each of five regions—one set in September and one in October. The September meetings for clergy and EMC committees dealt with the basic organization of the Every Member Canvass, the proposal-building procedures, the parish dinner, and the enlistment of team captains. At the October meetings we dealt with the enlistment and training of visitors and the Visitation Sunday procedures; and we recommended ways of doing an effective follow-up to the EMC.

In December we evaluated what had happened and agreed that we should continue this kind of training program another year. We also decided to write a better and more useful manual. The manual was written over the winter months so that we would be ready for an early start in May or June. It outlined a step-by-step EMC program we called the "Covenant Plan." The Covenant Plan is an accumulation of the thinking and experiences of many people over several years and is based on certain assumptions and theology which others may or may not accept.

One of these is the belief that we are responsible before God for the stewardship or the trusteeship of what he has given us. The import of this belief is that we are not responsible to the local vestry but to God for our stewardship. Therefore, if a person feels that the local parish is not doing anything significant with the money he has given, he is justified in withdrawing it from that parish and giving it some place else. Just as parishioners are responsible for the stewardship of what God has given them, so parishes are responsible for the stewardship of their funds. This means that as clergy and parish leaders we are accountable to God and our fellow parishioners for the way in which we use the resources given to us in trust—the time, talents, and money of the congregation.

As congregations, no less than as individuals, we are expected to be accountable. In a time when institutions and values are being challenged, the Church is not excused this scrutiny. Some of the long-established pressures for giving to the Church—such as fear, guilt, peer pressure—do not work anymore. The big question is: What difference does my giving make?

In a recent Harris survey, organized religion ranked fourth in a list of twelve institutions with the highest percentage of people who have confidence in these institutions. If we are to maintain the level of credibility that will encourage people to trust the Church with their resources, we must be accountable. Every EMC should therefore provide a process through which people of the congregation can be involved in the program decision-making process.

In the same way, all members of the congregation share the responsibility for the outreach of the parish in response to the mandate of Christ. It does not rest only on the shoulders of the rector and vestry, but on the whole People of God. A process should be found whereby parishioners can feel involved in that mission, not just so that they can share the responsibility, but since they are the People of God they have a right to feel a deep sense of being a part of that congregation. When we do not involve people in decision-making, or even report to them on what's being done, we are cutting them off from that sense of involvement in this great world movement of reconciliation and love.

Our stewardship teaching and programming must give people an opportunity to express their stewardship at the level of their understanding of what that means. T. A. Katonen in his book *A Theology for Christian Stewardship* identified four levels of stewardship response. The first is the level of law. At this level it is a response to conscience, duty, or social obligation which lays a claim on us requiring that we give something. There is nothing distinctly Christian in the giving, it is a response to a principle, not to a personal savior.

The second is the level of discipline. Here giving is orderly and systematic. The Christian life is strengthened by the discipline of regular giving. Giving at this level is part of the discipline of the Christian life.

The third is the level of concern. At this stage a new question about how much I should give emerges. Stewardship has moved from a response to obligation to an expression of concern.

The fourth is the level of grace. This is the point at which giving becomes a free-will offering. A personal relationship with God prompts an offering in love free from coercion, comparison, or any kind of self-interest.

In every congregation there are people who approach giving from one of these levels. In a state of perfection we might be able to finance the church on a simple appeal to faith and love. But the first three levels are also a part of Christian stewardship and they cannot be ignored. I am convinced that God blesses the widow's mite as much as the sacrifical gift of the millionaire, and that these two persons are not the same. There are different dynamics present on the decision to give which should be respected by the parish leaders. E. K. Lankester in his book *The Advancement of Science* (Saint Clair Shores, Michigan: Scholarly Press, 1890) says: "Nature gives no reply to general inquiry. She must be interrogated by questions that already contain the answers she is to give." It is the same with people, we are not challenged by general statements. The challenge should be couched in specifics, and sometimes even include the answer. Any EMC program should include a flexible approach which will encourage the response of people at all levels of stewardship. We cannot treat everyone alike.

The Every Member Canvass is a normal part of the parish program. It should not be seen as an optional extra or a special burden. To quote T. A. Kantonen again: "It is high time we examined stewardship from the point of view of the theology of the Gospel. A clear view of the intimate relation between evangelical theology and stewardship is of vital concern to both. Both have their starting point in an encounter with the living Christ. Theology seeks to think out the meaning of that encounter. Stewardship seeks to live it out. A theology that fails to relate itself to the vital issues of Christian activity shrivels into lifeless intellectualism, a sterile preoccupation with abstract concepts. And a stewardship that is not rooted in clear and sound theological convictions degenerates into shallow activism and loses its distinctive Christian character."

Like any other aspects of the Church program, effective stewardship requires planning and committed leadership. Nothing should be taught in this program which is in conflict with the central purpose of the Church, nothing should be done which has to be undone later.

Before choosing an EMC method or program, the vestry should decide what they want the EMC to accomplish. Programs are generally written with specific goals in mind and a bad match of method and goals generally ends in a frustrating experience for all concerned. If the goal is straight fund rais-

ing, the method will be different than if the goal is stewardship education; and while every annual EMC should include
both fund raising and stewardship education, the EMC committees often choose the method on the basis of what is comfortable rather than what will work. The old saying that
"money without mission is hopeless and mission without
money is hopeless" should be taken seriously by every parish
vestry.

The Covenant Plan is designed to accomplish four goals.
The first is "to develop a better understanding of Christian
stewardship." Stewardship is a popular subject among
people who are concerned about such things as the environment, the distribution of goods, and hunger. Stewardship is
an "in" word at the moment and we should build on that
interest to teach the Christian dimension of stewardship as it
applies to the Church and our lives day by day.

The second goal is "to develop a deeper concern for the
whole work of the Church," hoping that in some way the
Covenant Plan will help to break out of the "cocoonism"
which is crippling many of our parishes. Cocoonism can destroy our sense of mission and weaken the impact of the
Gospel on a world in need.

The third is "to encourage all members to make a financial
commitment to the work of the Church." The Covenant Plan
does not apologize in any way for the financial challenge, but
the real leadership for this challenge must come from the inside of the parish—the rector and vestry. The rector has to be
prepared to teach a standard of giving and qualify that teaching both theologically and scripturally. People are looking for
guidepost standards and a standard of giving is as important
to our total life and being as any other teaching. The principle
of proportionate giving is the foundation on which we can
build percentage giving. The modern tithe, five percent of
gross income, is an understandable standard, but many
people retain the biblical standard of ten percent—or even
more. We start by accepting the principle of proportionate
giving and go from there. This teaching and the subsequent
pace setting must come from the parish leadership.

The fourth goal is "to develop an active stewardship committee in every parish." This may not be a special or new committee; it could be written into the job description of one of the functioning committees or it could be done by the vestry. The idea is to have a group which will carry forward the stewardship concerns and learnings on a year-round basis.

The step-by-step process outlined in the Covenant Plan manual is relatively simple and forms the basic building blocks of any well-organized Every Member Canvass. The first step, after the EMC committee is appointed, is to work up a plan of action or proposal for the coming year. That is, a proposed program which has been developed by the people themselves. We do this by getting together a representative group from the parish to dream and think about what they want the parish to be, what should be the parish priorities and so on. We ask such questions as: "If the local religion editor of the paper were writing a story on your parish, what would you like him to be able to say?" We have found that a representative group in the parish often has greater dreams and expectations than the vestry realizes. The vestry is so occupied with just keeping the nuts and bolts of the parish together they do not always have time to be creative.

The second step is to communicate that plan of action or proposed program to the parishioners in every way possible. This includes the use of pew leaflets, articles in the parish newsletter and public press, special speakers, a parish dinner, and any other ways creative people can develop. There is a heavy emphasis on involving people in the stewardship program, as well as making sure that everyone in the parish knows what is going on. Involving people is a common strategy in fund raising, but it should go on all the time in the body of Christ so some of the opportunities of involvement generated by the EMC may have long-term good results of community building in the parish. If communication to any one part of the body is cut off, that part of the body begins to die. It is a corporate responsibility within the parish to make sure parishioners feel they are a part of the Church body. This applies to those on the edges of regular parish activities as well as to the regular worshipers and workers.

The fourth step is to give the people of the parish an opportunity to respond to Christ's teaching about giving and the financial challenge being laid out before them by the parish. Experience has shown that home visits are the most effective way of doing this. However, since in some parishes every home is not visited, the Covenant Plan has built-in options to home visiting. Many options have been tried, with greater or lesser success, as a change of pace, but none have the lasting quality of home visits. In our training meetings we try to advise people what to look out for if they choose to use any of these options.

Other parishes accept the Covenant Plan as a guide, but do not follow the plan faithfully. That is, they pick and choose what pieces of it they want to use. While the manual is a self-help book which will help local committees do a better EMC even if they only use parts of it, the difficulty of picking pieces of a number of different programs and putting them together is that they do not necessarily fit, with the result that you end up with a very disjointed EMC program, a series of steps with no cohesiveness. The results have not been as good as in the parishes where they used the full Covenant Plan.

The Covenant Plan has proven to be very successful in parishes where it was used faithfully. The results were good in terms of both financial return and overall parish life. There was an average pledged increase of twenty-one percent in parishes where they visited every home, with an average increase of twelve percent in parishes where they did *not* visit every home. Over half of the parishes experienced an increase in church attendance and most reported an improvement in congregation morale. There was a general feeling of success and a more positive attitude toward the work of the church.

For most of us, the Every Member Canvass is synonymous with raising money. It has many side benefits which are shortchanged by our desire to get the EMC over as fast as possible with as little effort or exposure as possible. There is a verse in St. Paul's letter to the Corinthians (II Cor.8:8) which all Canvass committees should read and meditate upon. As

Paul told the Corinthians of the giving of the Macedonians for
the poor in Jerusalem, he ended his account of their generosity and sacrifice by saying "This is not an order, but I am putting your love to the test." He then went on to say the challenge for people to give of themselves to Christ and his
Church is not given with any legislative authority, but it is a
testing of their priorities and their love. None of us like to
have our love challenged, so it is natural that people react in a
variety of ways. The EMC program should include the kind of
teaching, community support, and sensitivity which help
people to grow in the midst of that kind of challenge.

Betty Pearson

Betty Pearson is an incredible person —and I use the adjective advisedly. I ought to know. We've known each other since childhood. Betty has served as a consultant to clergy groups in several dioceses. She is a trainer for the Alabama Plan, past president of the Episcopal Churchwomen of Mississippi, a member of the Mississippi Advisory Committee of the Civil Rights Commission, and was an invaluable member of our Chicago "101" team. I know of no person for whom I have more respect —or greater affection. At the Province IV Stewardship Workshop in Jacksonville, Betty accosted me with, "Oscar, I'm tired of all these church conferences with no women on the program! You've got to do something about that!" Grasping for a response, I asked, "Why don't you write a chapter for our proposed stewardship book?" This chapter is the very happy result.

The Mississippi Method

THE 1975 Annual Council of the Diocese of Mississippi passed a resolution authorizing the bishop to appoint a diocesan stewardship committee, which would be charged with "the responsibility of informing itself of the principles of stewardship and of the very best methods of implementing those principles, and of promoting those principles and methods throughout the diocese." This is a description of the diocesan program of stewardship help for congregations that this committee has developed, and of some of the things we've learned along the way.

The committee members began their work by studying and discussing the theology of good Christian stewardship, and learning as much as possible about a variety of different approaches to a stewardship program. The Stewardship Workshop sponsored by the Office of Development at the provincial level was extremely helpful both in acquainting committee members with some of these approaches, and in increasing their understanding of the theology.

The diocesan stewardship program is based on the following assumptions:

1. Good diocesan stewardship grows out of good stewardship at the parochial level, so the committee's first task would be to offer help to the parishes and missions.

2. The basis for any program should be a sound biblical and Christian theology of money and giving, and this theology is defined in *Stewardship: Myth and Methods* by John MacNaughton (New York: Seabury Press, 1975), which should be promoted as a study guide throughout the diocese.

3. There are many effective methods of promoting good stewardship, and rather than developing a single "Mississippi Plan," the committee would offer help with a variety of methods that were consistent with the biblical theology.

The process that has developed begins with a request for help from a parish or mission to the chairman of the diocesan Stewardship Committee. In response to that request a member of the committee goes to the church for an exploratory meeting with the vestry. At this meeting the concerns and questions of the vestry are answered, the biblical theology of stewardship is discussed, and there is a brief description of each of the methods with which the diocese can offer help. These include the MacNaughton Plan, the Alabama Plan, the Covenant Plan, and a combination of one or more of these designed for the particular parish. In addition, if the vestry wants to use a professional fund raiser, the committee will recommend one whose method is consistent with the theology.

The MacNaughton and Covenant Plans can be used by the parish using just the printed material, or with a consultant to help with the planning and the caller training. The Alabama Plan, or an individually designed plan, requires the use of an outside consultant.

At this initial meeting, the representative from the stewardship committee might also help the vestry diagnose the present giving pattern of the parish, and discuss specific problem areas. His purpose is to serve as a resource to the vestry, giving them as much information as possible that will help them in developing a good stewardship program, and in choosing the method that seems best for them.

Following this meeting, the vestry may decide that it can conduct the stewardship program with no further help from the diocese. If, however, the decision is made to use an outside consultant, the chairman of the stewardship committee gives the vestry the names of the diocesan consultants qualified to work with the method or plan chosen. Choosing and contacting the consultant are the responsibility of the local church.

Two things helped us get this program underway in a short period of time: we already had a pool of trained diocesan consultants who were doing vestry goal-settings and vacancy consultations, and with very little additional training they could begin to do stewardship consultations; and one of the originators of the Alabama Plan moved back into this diocese, which enabled us to train additional consultants in the Alabama Plan by using the apprentice system.

Our experience has been that while it is possible for a church to conduct its own Every Member Canvass, the best results have followed the use of a consultant. This is especially true in churches which are having a pre-budget canvass for the first time. We have also learned that the exploratory meeting is in itself a short stewardship consultation, and there has been a very positive response from the churches that have had such a meeting, even when they have not asked for any additional help with their stewardship program.

One of the biggest problems has been that most vestries

don't think about asking for help with stewardship until just
before Every Member Canvass time, and this is much too late
to plan a good parish stewardship program, so we are looking
for ways to publicize the work of the committee, emphasizing
the necessity of having the exploratory meeting early in the
year.

This diocesan program gives a parish or mission church
that is looking for help with stewardship a wide variety of
good plans from which to choose, and the differences between them—which are largely a matter of emphasis, EMC
methodology, or the choice of using or not using an outside
consultant—make it possible to find the plan which best suits
the particular situation in each church. In spite of the differences in method, there are at least five important elements
that are common to any good stewardship program, whether
it is one of the prepackaged kits, or a do-it-yourself model.
These are:

1. Theology
2. Purpose
3. EMC Plan
4. Training of Callers
5. Evaluation and Follow-up

In the different models for parish stewardship programs
one or the other of these elements will be given greater or
lesser emphasis, and the methods used to implement them
will be different, and it is these differences that enable each
parish to find a good "fit." More important, regardless of the
plan used, are the more subtle implications of the five elements, the often unexpressed and unrecognized ways in
which they can affect the total life of the parish.

I

The Theology

This article is not meant to be a statement of a biblical theology of money but an attempt to explore some of the implica-

tions of a commitment to such a theology, so it can simply be said in preface that any good stewardship program will be based on the understanding that all things come from God, and that one gives out of thanksgiving in proportion to what one has been given, and out of one's own deep need to give. The importance of the theological basis means that a good stewardship program must also be a good Christian education program, and that growth in stewardship comes from teaching, preaching, and witnessing to the theology. There must be opportunities for the members of the congregation not only to hear the theology, but to explore its meaning for their own lives, in an atmosphere of open and nonjudgmental sharing.

Of the published stewardship plans, the MacNaughton book has an especially clear and easy-to-read discussion of the theological basis of Christian stewardship, and is a good book for group study, whether used as a preliminary to the MacNaughton EMC plan, or with one of the other methods. Other books and tapes are available for group and individual study, but the best teacher is the person who already has an understanding of and commitment to the theology, and can make a personal witness to it.

What are some of the implications for the parish of a commitment to this theology? First, perhaps, is that it means having a prebudget canvass, since we will be giving to God and not to a church budget. The needs for Christian ministry are boundless, and cannot be limited by a predetermined budget.

Another is that our attitude toward money will change, and we will begin to understand money as a sacrament. This will help us break down the man-made division between the sacred and the secular, and between money and finances as the layman's forte, and spiritual concerns as the clergy's.

When the use of money is seen as sacramental, we can begin to have a better understanding of the theological implications of all that we say and do, and to articulate and share those implications. We all yearn for ways in which to make life more meaningful, and this kind of looking for and sharing the connection between theological truths and our life experiences is a way, perhaps the best way, to find meaning in ordinary events. Good stewardship teaches us that theology and experience are interdependent: what we do grows out of what we believe; what we believe grows out of what we do.

Another result is that our feelings about our own giving and the giving of others will change. A stewardship program that has a sound theological basis is a program of education and witness, and avoids the two extremes that often result from a hard-sell fund raising program: the people who don't increase their giving, or who can't meet a goal set for them by someone else, feel guilty, while those who do feel self-righteous. When we understand that since all we are and have belongs to God, none of us can ever give enough, but each of us is at a different place in the process of growth in good stewardship, we can be freed of the burden of both guilt and self-righteousness.

And finally, the parish that takes the theology seriously will have to take giving outside the parish seriously. Some of the consultants using the Alabama Plan, for example, ask the vestry to set a goal of giving one dollar for work outside the congregation for every dollar spent within it. Even if the EMC plan does not ask for such a specific goal, the same principles that apply to individual giving will help the congregation to grow in its understanding of the need to give outside itself. And the parish or diocese that gives generously outside itself will have exciting things going on inside.

II

The Purpose

One of the greatest dangers of a well-planned Every Member Canvass is that it is certain to be successful. Regardless of the method, if the plan is followed there will be an increase in pledges, sometimes slight, but often as high as fifty or sixty percent. A good plan, efficiently carried through, works; and the danger in this certainty of success, and the reason for looking at purpose, is that we can so easily equate increased giving with increased ministry. A big jump in pledges can mean increased salaries, new choir robes, a comfortable contingency fund, and perhaps a new building program. None of these things is bad in itself, but unless the success of the EMC is also measured in terms of an increase in ministry to the needs of others, we will have confused a balanced budget with good stewardship.

The EMC begins, then, with the vestry or a special long-range planning committee seeking answers to such questions as:"What is our purpose? Why are we having an EMC? To what and for what are people being asked to pledge?" If the Church takes seriously its definition as the body of Christ, questions like these quickly go beyond the issue of having a balanced budget and maintaining the status quo, and the question of the purpose of the EMC becomes: "What is the ministry of Christ that can and should be done through this church?" The stewardship program should offer an opportunity for the congregation to "dream"; that is, to project all the possibilities for ministry through this church, and then to define those dreams in terms of specific things that could be done with the full use of the financial resources and the time and talents of the congregation.

This projection of the possibilities for ministry accomplishes several things. It moves the congregation past the limits of last year's budget. Without setting a precanvass budget, it meets the need of the giver to know what he is being asked to give for. It becomes the data for planning parish program when the time comes to set the budget. And most important, it makes the essential connection between fund raising and Christian ministry, so that good stewardship is understood as including both the *giving* of money, and the *doing* of God's work.

The success of the well-planned EMC will be seen, not just in increased pledges but in a renewed atmosphere of fellowship, sharing, enthusiasm, and involvement. However, this will gradually dwindle away if it becomes apparent that nothing has really changed. The stewardship program that mobilizes the financial and human resources of the congregation also has the responsibilities of offering opportunities for using those resources in real Christian ministry.

Care must be taken to keep this an honest projection of the possibilities and opportunities for ministry, and not let it become manipulative by being an indirect way to set a precanvass budget, or a way to "hook" people on a program.

III

The EMC Plan

The success of the canvass depends on having a well-structured and efficiently followed plan. No matter what the level of giving in the parish has been in the past, asking for pledges by mailing out cards or announcing a pledge Sunday simply does not get the job done. A good EMC means a lot of hard work, attention to details, and personal visits by trained callers. Both the MacNaughton and Covenant books outline an EMC plan in detail, and can be followed step by step or adjusted to fit particular situations. (Caution: changing a plan, or using part of one plan with part of another, will not be successful without an understanding of the rationale of the plans, the way in which the pieces fit together.)

An EMC plan is a detailed, step-by-step process, and it must be followed faithfully, but with imagination. Therefore, the choice of a chairman or chairwoman is a crucial one. There must also be a real commitment to the underlying theology, as well as to the particular method, on the part of the parish leadership. The Alabama Plan spells out this necessary commitment by requiring that the rector be personally committed to proportionate giving, with the goal of tithing; that the vestry adopt the principle of proportionate giving, both as individuals and for the parish; and that at least twenty-five percent of the family units in the congregation participate in the training sessions.

A good Every Member Canvass plan will include:

1.   Diagnosis—an analysis of the present pledging pattern. This does not have to be complicated but should give a clear picture of "where we are now."

2.   A calendar of events—beginning in early spring (for a fall campaign) when the chairperson is selected and a contract is made with a consultant, if one is to be used, and going beyond the actual canvass to include evaluation and follow-up.

3.   A method for selecting, training, and assigning callers.

4.   A system for handling the mechanics of the canvass, and who will be responsible for doing what, including such things as mail-outs, publicity, parish dinners and other programs, sermons and talks on stewardship, keeping track of the pledge cards, receiving the cards and making records, and "cleaning up" all calls within a definite deadline.

5.   Plans for reporting the results of the canvass to the congregation.

6.   An evaluation of the canvass, and plans for follow-up.

To participate in an Every Member Canvass is an opportunity for personal growth in faith, as well as an opportunity for service, and one of the goals of the EMC plan should be the involvement of all the age groups in the parish. The skills learned in planning and managing a good canvass can be used in planning and carrying out other parish programs. An EMC that is a success story increases the congregation's confidence in its own resources, human and financial, and generates enthusiasm and involvement that can revitalize all aspects of parish life.

IV

Training the Callers

One of the keys to the success of an EMC is having callers who know what they are expected to do, when and how; who have the infomation they will need to answer questions about the Church; and who are themselves committed to porportionate giving. No one should serve as a canvass caller who will not agree to participate in the training sessions.

In selecting callers, consideration should be given to using young people, and both women and men of all ages. Young people can contribute imagination and enthusiasm in the areas of publicity and ideas for parish dinners and other meetings. They often can make the most effective witnesses to the meaning of Christ in their lives.

The following suggestions for the training of callers are based on the Alabama Plan, which is especially strong in this area for several reasons. It emphasizes theological education, and as much time is spent on theology as on method. It is longer than most training plans (two three-hour sessions) which gives the participants time to explore their own commitment, as well as to be briefed on the mechanics of the canvass. It increases involvement by requiring that twenty-five percent of the family units be represented at the training sessions. However, since the decision to be a caller is not made until the end of the training, it gives more people an opportunity to discuss the theology and explore their own feelings about giving without having to first agree to serve as a caller.

The training of callers should cover two broad areas:

1.   The theology. An EMC canvass through personal calls is a "witness" model, a way to share one's faith with another person. The training should include both a formal presentation of the theology of Christian stewardship and an opportunity for the participants to increase their own commitment and gain skills in sharing that commitment.

2.   The mechanics. The callers need to be sure that they understand what is expected of them and what their deadlines are. They must be given the information they might need to answer questions. The training should include a discussion of manner and behavior in making a call, as well as an opportunity to practice making a canvass call.

The standard for callers is to be open and nondefensive. Consider having the callers go alone rather than in teams. Calling in pairs gives the callers a feeling of security, perhaps, but it also puts pressure on both the "call-ee" ("two against one") and the callers ("Am I doing this the way my partner thinks I ought to do it?"). There will be a more open and honest sharing of the faith on a one-to-one basis. It is important that everyone in the congregation, including the rector and the canvassers, be called on. No one should be denied the opportunity of meeting God through a caller.

At the close of the training sessions, people are asked to sign up to be callers. No one who feels uncomfortable in the role, or who has been coerced into "volunteering," can be an effective caller. Only the person who has a personal commitment to the theology of Christian stewardship can be an honest and effective witness to that theology. So it is important to be faithful to the standard that it is OK *not* to volunteer to be a caller.

Beyond the immediate effect on the canvass, there are at least two other important implications for the parish in this kind of intensive caller training. The first is that a substantial proportion of the congregation will have participated in what is essentially good Christian education, a short course in the theology of stewardship. This can be the beginning of a continuing program of education and training for the lay ministry. The second is that training people in the skills needed to make canvass calls also increases their skills and their interest in other kinds of calls. The church can become a "calling parish" all during the year, and not just during the Every Member Canvass.

The response of people who have participated in these training sessions has been that the training is of tremendous value to them personally, increasing their commitment to the parish, deepening their understanding of stewardship, and giving them new and satisfying opportunities for ministry.

V

Evaluation and Follow-up.

This is one of the most important elements in a good stewardship program, and the one most often neglected. At the end of a successful EMC, when the committee has worked long and hard, there is the understandable temptation to heave a sigh of relief, congratulate one another on a job well done, and say "that's that until next year." But it is only when this final step is accomplished that the stewardship program can become a year-round part of the church's life.

An evaluation of the Every Member Canvass gives the congregation an opportunity to share what they have learned from the experience, and to make plans for the future; and it is only through a planned follow-up that the gains of a successful EMC, the ideas and energies generated, can be plugged into a parish program of ministry. If it is true for an individual that "an unexamined life is not worth living," it is no less true for the church. The parish community learns and grows to the measure of its willingness to reflect on the collective experience, to be open to the need for change, to respond to its opportunities for ministry, and to witness through action its commitment to the theology of Christian stewardship.

The Covenant Plan lists some ideas for follow-up, and the Alabama Plan includes an evaluation and follow-up session with the consultant, but there remains a real need for developing and sharing models to help congregations build on the gains of a successful EMC, and to understand the EMC as just one step in a year-round stewardship program.

In the fall of 1972 and the spring of 1973, the Executive Council visited all of the dioceses in the Church to gather information on program and budget, and the response was the same in almost every diocese: the priorities were Christian education and evangelism. Although there may be no obvious connection, experience has taught us that a good stewardship program is also a program of evangelism and of Christian education. Is stewardship just one way to approach the issues of evangelism and Christian education, or were we really asking for stewardship help all the time and not knowing it? Perhaps the truth is that good stewardship is so basic to the Christian life style that it will inevitably lead to growth in all areas of our lives, both as individuals and as a Church.

We are finding effective ways to help parish and mission

churches develop sound stewardship programs. The challenge now is to develop strategies for promoting good stewardship practices at the diocesan and national levels, so that we can be consistently faithful to the biblical and theological principles of good stewardship at every level of the Church's life, from the giving of an individual to the setting of a national budget.

Arthur Ben Chitty

When Arthur Ben Chitty was asked to head the fund raising campaign in his Sewanee parish, his first experience, he replied, "I will only take the job if you double your goal!" They did. It worked. That was a long time ago. To most of us who know him, Arthur is "Mr. Sewanee," having headed its promotional office for twenty years. As president of the Association of Episcopal Colleges, Arthur has identified more wealthy Episcopalians than anyone else in the Church. His statistics astound most listeners. "There are about 5,000 genuine multimillionnaires in the Episcopal Church. They attend only 200 parishes, and although characteristically philanthropic, are rarely challenged by Church causes. Although twenty-three of the sixty-six "super rich" listed by Fortune were Episcopalians, their record for giving to the Church is abysmally low. In fact, if every Episcopalian went on welfare and tithed his check, the Church's income would double!" Arthur's overriding hobby is history, and Who's Who credits him with being on a half dozen national boards. He probably knows more than any living person about Sewanee and our Episcopal colleges. Despite all his commitments, he still finds time to help us by sharing his knowledge about stewardship. I, personally, and the Church at large are in his debt.

Organizing a Parish For Stewardship

NO PARISH should attempt to raise money until its philosophy is clear. The people must understand *why* the money is sought.

Since our money is part of us (representing our effort and talent) and since by and through money we *act*—for good or bad—the ends for which our funds are used become direct expressions of our character, our hopes, or our weaknesses.

Having, by the study of scripture and by application of its principles to modern living, established a clear philosophy of stewardship, we turn to its implementation. To study fund raising methods before we know the philosophy is like manufacturing an explosive without knowing what we plan to use it for.

Three ingredients for a parish are Pastor, People, and Plant. Some might put People before Pastor but all would agree that Plant is least important. Under Plant comes equipment, and fund raising involves its use.

Besides typewriter, telephone, mimeograph, dictating machine, PA system, bulletin board, filing cabinets, safe, tape recorder, tract rack, poster material, mailing permit, and so on, there are two special needs for parish fund raising which many overlook. They are an addressing system and a basic, permanent parish record system. The addressing system may involve one of the stencil systems, access to a computer system, or merely the carbon or chemical duplicating of address labels. But there must be some fairly simple way to get a message to the whole parish in a hurry and at minimum expense.

The parish record system requires more discussion.

Every parish should have, periodically, a printed or mimeographed directory of its members. Beyond this, however, it is vital to have a card system which records the dates of birth, baptism, confirmation; full name, relationships to other members of the parish, place of birth, parish from which transferred, means of livelihood, address, phone number, and names of children.

It is highly important that gift information also be kept in accessible form. It is a moot point whether the individual weekly gifts should be posted on the permanent record card. I think not. The treasurer usually needs his separate set of records on which he can post weekly returns from envelopes. The permanent card should record the individual's or family's annual rate of giving and any special gifts—a large donation to a general building fund, for example, or the gift of a stained glass window.

Why should this be done? God knows what the individual has done, and isn't that enough?

The succeeding rector will find this type of record most helpful. It could furnish crucial information in a guidance problem, and it is a way of showing gratitude. We know where Dante, one of the world's greatest theologians, placed the ingrate. The display of gratitude is a positive virtue. To record for posterity the generosity of an individual is a good thing. Finally, this information is most important for the future stewardship committee; the benefactions of the future will come largely from those who have given in the past.

Every parish should also have a file on memorial gifts. Before it has been forgotten there should be a record made, either in a memorial book or in a permanent card system, or both, of the donor of the candlesticks, the cruets, the chalice, the altar hangings, and so on. Where possible, these should be appropriately marked. It is important in the continuity of a parish for those who worship today to realize how much they owe to those who have gone before.

Records are tremendously important, and it is surprising how few parishes have them. One may not *find* records in a parish, but there will be a special place in heaven for those who *leave* them. So much for records.

Before we discuss procedures, let us consider human resources.

The talents in a parish, even a small parish, are truly surprising. If a clergyman would double, triple, quadruple—or increase a thousandfold—his effectiveness in God's work, let him collect (on his record cards) the talents, hobbies, and special interests of his parishioners. It is the easiest thing in the world to do. Questioning a communicant about his special interests is one of the most helpful aids to early parochial visitation. Unless a record is made of these potential assets they are forgotten and may never be used in God's service. Even if the clergyman has an unusual mental filing system and instantaneous recall, he takes it all with him when he moves, retires, or drops dead in his tracks. His successor will bless him if he has jotted down on the permanent record card the fact that John Smith loves to operate a slide rule and that Jane Jones enjoys making beautiful drapes. Every time a parishioner can use his special talent in the service of his church, he is a better communicant. Ben Franklin was not the first to point out that we make friends by asking people to do something for us, preferably something easy at first, and then thanking them heartily. Many of these talents can be utilized in the stewardship program of a parish. Canvass carefully the talents of women who formerly worked, women whose children are grown, and men who are retired.

There are two general types of fund raising in a parish. There is the occasional need for a capital fund effort (new building, extension, or major renovation), and there is the year-to-year effort to make meaningful a plan of systematic giving. The first is usually, though not always, a self-centered effort, and the second usually, though not always, is our avenue for "outside" or "totally unselfish" giving. There is no reason why this pattern has to obtain. We can stage special, large-scale efforts for a missionary cause in Liberia. We can include capital building programs in our annual canvass.

Here are some general rules and observations.

1.   The only really dependable rule is that there are no rules.

2.   Money is not unclean. The clergyman who thinks he should not become involved in fund raising either must redefine fund raising (try stewardship) or must conclude that he doesn't really believe the Lord's work is important.

3.   A reasonable constituency of a parish extends beyond its membership roster. There are good citizens, unchurched, who want to help. There are descendants and relatives of parishioners.

4.   Few people give to their utmost.

5.   Practically no one who gives generously regrets it.

6.   Today the canvass represents practically the only pretext on which the busy man can be induced to practice

genuine Christian missionary effort. He won't preach from a barrell top, he won't go out seeking lost souls, he won't presume to speak out against individual immorality, he won't even ask a friend to come to church. But he *will* solicit for the Every Member Canvass. It is respectable. It is accepted. He does it for the Red Cross and for the Elks. Make his soliciting experience as meaningful as you can, because you don't have him in that position under many other circumstances.

7.   There are two ways of balancing a budget; cutting expenses and increasing income. The great parish takes the latter route.

8.   The clergyman who "protects" his people from other fund raisers (the bishop, the missionary, the school, or the university) defeats himself and harms them. Rather he should give them every channel for the expression of their philanthropic impulses to further God's work to the limit of their capacities. Giving begets giving. The person who gives to his university is apt to give more, not less, to his parish.

9.   The healthy spirit of a parish can be sensed. It is real and recognizable.

10.   "Give until it hurts" is the PR man at his worst. "Give until it feels good" is a valid appeal. If you give enough in the right way, it will feel good.

11.   The impulse to give to "outside" causes is not instinctive. It is a cultivated reaction. It is the product of education, endless persuasion.

12.   A rector continually faces a choice of taking either the talent most readily available or the best talent. Other things being equal, take the latter.

13.   In matching persons who will call and those on whom they will call, remember that the man who gives generously can make a very effective persentation to another in his approximate income bracket who gives less.

14.   Witnessing is sound—theologically and psychologically—if it is devoid of pride. It is no more than fair play for the visitor (canvasser or solicitor) to tell what he himself is giving. Indeed it is unfair *not* to, since he is going to know the amount of his canvassee's pledge. Remember that Christ an-

nounced publicly both the identity and the amount given by the widow who offered her mite.

15. To limit the concept of stewardship to mere money-giving or money-getting is as cynical as comparing the Holy Communion to mere eating and drinking.

Tithing is the most easily defended standard for steward-ship. It has scriptural authority and it makes practical sense. What is a tithe?

The House of Bishops in 1949 said in effect that the circum-stances of our modern life and its organized ramifications led them to define the Christian tithe as the minimum standard of charitable giving, with at least five percent of that tithe des-ignated for the parish church.

Many think there are wide variations in the calculating of a tithe. I agree. Some might with propriety—certainly as an ini-tial goal—consider it to be ten percent of income after taxes. Some who start with this calculation end by using the gross income figure. Some might calculate a fair market value of clothes given to a rummage sale as part of a tithe. A doctor certainly should consider free services rendered as part of his humanitarian practice, but he should remember that a living Church has daily needs. If we all made our full tithes directly to the needy, the Church would die and there would be no one left to teach tithing. Against this we must concede that the Church is *not* going to die and that the individual must consider his personal need to give.

It is a very effective device to have two sides or two colors of pledge cards. The person is asked to "sign on the black side if the gift is a tithe and on the red side if it is not." Another way of dramatizing the tithe is to ask for unsigned question-naires from all members, on which is computed (by the parishioner) what the amount of a tithe would be for him if he gave it. This would show the vestry what the parish income would be if everyone tithed. It would dramatize the impor-tance of stewardship education.

The people must be told: "The Church does not ask for your money—it asks for *you.*" The Church will not close or the diocese disintegrate or the bishops retire to other pursuits if you do not give. However, the effect upon *you* can well be catastrophic if you turn your back on God's call. The consequences are the warping of your soul through rationalizations, attempts to justify a selfish position. We hear "I don't like the rector—don't approve of the bishops—don't like high church. These are irrelevant and untrue. The truth is "pocketbook protection." *Your need* to give just as you *need* to worship, to pray, to ask forgiveness, and to be forgiven. These are psychically based religious needs which are universal.

It is a shock to realize that the average Every Member Canvass or the successful drive for a parish house can defeat real stewardship. How? When the circumstances are such that the person making the gift is not sacrificing, then the requirements of stewardship are not met. A gift to your own parish house is somewhat like buying a nice piece of furniture for your home. A gift to enable Christian education for your children is somewhat like hiring a tutor. Such gifts are certainly not bad, but if they are the only kind of gifts made, they do not qualify the donor as a good steward.

We have become conditioned to thinking of our giving as purchasing—satisfaction, tax deductions, services for ourselves and our family—and to the extent that our giving involves this kind of a bargain, it is defeating the purpose of stewardship. These are ugly connotations and must be softened by charitable interpretation of motives. We fallible mortals are not permitted to condemn our fellows on a basis of inward motives which we cannot know. A donor must in all circumstances be credited with the best intentions. His true stewardship is between him and God.

Finally, although a gift to a good cause is commendable under almost any circumstances, it becomes holy in the sight of God when it is given with humble prayer.

Good stewardship can be faith in action—a special kind of worship.

PART THREE

Selected Sermons

John B. Coburn

There is no way I'll ever forget John Coburn's words, "Oscar, the Development Committee would like you to resign from the Executive Council, move Billie and the family from Mississippi to Manhattan, and set up the Development Office for the Church." If it weren't for that beginning, this book would not exist! Mainly because of the "heavy hand" of one of the most respected theologians in our Church, I was unable to turn the challenge down. In spite of the trauma and cultural shock of the transition, Billie and I will be eternally grateful for the opportunities it has brought us. None is more important, however, than to know, respect, and love John and Ruth Coburn as dear, dear friends.

Stewardship and the Communion of Saints

With men it is impossible, but not with God; for all things are possible with God.

Mark 10:27

WHAT can be said about money that has not already been said? What can be said about death that has not already been said? What can be said about money and death that may provide life?

This is a day when we think about money because it is the day in which the stewardship program for the year 1974 begins at St. James Church. It is also the Sunday after All Saints' Day when we think of those who have died whom we have loved and who have loved us, and who now live in their love for us as in ours for them, joined together with them in what is called the Communion of Saints.

So together, those two themes form the theme of the day. That theme is: What you trust is what you become. Trust giving more than getting and you become a giving person. Trust love more than life itself and you become a living, loving person. Trust God with your giving and with your loves and you enter immediately into his kingdom; you participate directly in the Communion of Saints now. Saint Mark puts it very bluntly in the Gospel that was read this morning: if you put your trust in riches, you cannot enter into God's kingdom. If you put your trust in God, you can.

The rule of God's kingdom is to trust the Ruler. He is the Ruler. Trust him and then you have freedom to live a life of your own, giving and loving. If you are a rich man and you put your trust in your money, you inevitably become a person holding on to your possessions, building them up, holding on to yourself, building yourself up, and increasingly, therefore, becoming possessed by what you possess and by yourself—increasingly possessed by yourself.

You have met the kind, haven't you? Those men and women who are incapable of ever looking at life from any perspective except their own—their own position, their own wealth, their own family, their own loves. They are encrusted with their own possessions and, therefore, since they will never let them go, they cannot ever let themselves go into the mainstream of life.

It is one thing to see the Gospel validated by life, validated by our own experiences in life. It is relatively easy to see the Gospel validated in this way, in such an obvious way, by what happens to people who hold on to their money—and to see the contrary validated, to see what happens to people who are generous of spirit. Givers are generous of spirit and misers tend to become miserable. It is exactly the same thing with regard to another principle of God's kingdom—that is, with regard to love and the holding on to love, and the holding on to our loved ones who have died. You can become as preoccupied and obsessed with grief as you can with money. When you hold on to your loved ones and will not let them go, either in this life or into the life to come, you become obsessed with them and with your own loss.

To love is to give. To give away freely those whom you have already lost by death is to set them free, to give them new life so that they are then able to go about their new existence fully and freely. Once you have been able to do this with those whom you love, you discover that you are able to set yourself free to go about your own life fully and freely. They have their destiny, once they have died, and if we love them—if we truly love *them* and not our love of them, which is a form of self-love—we shall support them with our love and prayers as they go about fulfilling that destiny; going, as that wonderful Collect says, "from strength to strength in God's heavenly kingdom."

We do this more easily and more naturally when we trust God to take them into himself rather than trusting ourselves and the worth of our love. We do this more easily by trusting God than by any other way. To do this—that is, to commit them directly into God's care—is what we call participating in the Communion of Saints. It is affirming that the spirit of love which is revealed to us in God is the Eternal Spirit in which all people live finally, and where all people live most fully and most freely. Therefore, it is to set them free and to set ourselves free so that we can go about the business of fulfilling our destinies—loving, supporting, undergirding, loosing all those whom we love. To love another person is to set that person free to be himself or herself. We express that love in supporting that person to become who he or she is meant to become. When we can do that we are already living in God's kingdom—and that kingdom includes both life before death and life after death. To hold on to our own loved ones and to possess them is to destroy them. To set them free to become themselves under God is to emancipate them. Love is the steady direction of our will to loosen them from ourselves and to will their good.

This kind of giving is not so easy. It really is not possible for people to do this. Our self-love and our involvement with those whom we love is so great that we cannot easily do this. But with God all things are possible: the giving of money in a generous spirit; the giving over to him of those whom we love in a generous spirit; putting our trust neither in our riches nor in ourselves but in God—or in life itself or in love itself or in the simple process of giving away. That involves sacrifice at times and always a willingness not to possess, not to insist on having one's own way, not to be God with anybody's life. It is not easy, but when we have eyes to see beneath the surface of life and what moves in other people's lives, when we examine them and look searchingly into our own hearts, we see that at the core of the universe, at the heart of the experience of men and women, is this process which empowers people to live most fully as they give themselves. Those who live greatly give greatly. Those who live greatly are those who live loving lives—not the tight-fisted, miserable ones.

This process, this principle, which we can experience in some measure in our own lives and which is validated by the experiences we have in our own lives, is the principle that was lived most fully by Jesus Christ. He was the one who set forth in his life, death, and resurrection the principle of sacrifice, and of love's willingness to sacrifice, of God's willingness, wanting to love. And that love always prevails. What we cannot do, that which is impossible for us, God can do, because all things are possible with God, and therefore in him all our loves and all our lives prevail.

So the theme is a very simple one: give money and you will live; love people and you will live; trust God and you will live. Life is all of a piece, and it's all held together at its heart, in Christ in whom we and all whom we love live fully and freely both in this life and in the life to come. Amen.

Hugh McCandless

While rector of the Church of the Epiphany in Manhattan, Hugh McCandless gave stewardship training and education his highest priority. My friend, Lee Belford, Director of the Graduate School of Religion at New York University and associate priest at Epiphany says, "During Hugh's tenure of service—over a quarter century—the contributions to the parish increased bountifully and an endowment fund of $1,000,000 was created in the last decade." In retirement, as Rector Emeritus of Epiphany, Dr. McCandless continues to share his stewardship talents through a professional organization that aids congregations of all denominations. We are honored to have in this book a sermon of his choosing.

The Meaning of Stewardship

THIS NEXT WEEK letters will go out to the members and friends of this parish inviting them to subscribe to the maintenance of the work of the Church through this parish. About twenty people gave direct help in composing and compiling the material in these letters; about twenty more helped stuff and stamp the envelopes. This represents a large contribution in hours and effort to the work of this church. Now we hope and pray for an even bigger piece of work: that everyone who receives this letter will give twenty minutes of his time to reading it thoughtfully, and making his own decision prayerfully. In the face of today's conditions and today's costs, and in the light of this church's needs and its opportunities for service, we need subscriptions that are realistic. You will want to make a subscription that is really representative of your hopes for the church. Please make your decision slowly and carefully and prayerfully.

In recent years, this aspect of our church life has been called "stewardship." This word is common in the Bible. A steward was a housemanager for a king or a great lord. Since the Church is the household of God, its people are both the family of God, with privileges, and the servants of God, with responsibilities.

St. Paul says, "It is required of stewards that they be found faithful." (I Cor. 4:2) Of course, churchgoing and church support are central to faithful stewardship. Those who claim to be too broadminded to attend any church, or too spiritual to support any church, are either missing the point or evading it. Of course God is everywhere, but if we do not seek him and try to serve him somewhere, we shall find him nowhere. Since true worship is partly our offering of ourselves, sincere worship will make us want to implement that offering in some very definite way. It is a sound instinct of worship that has gradually led to the inclusion of a money offering as a vital part of every main church service. It is a definite gesture of response to God's challenging goodness to us. It is a response to his holiness. He made all material things for our use, so they are sacred. He makes many things sacramental so that he can give himself to us in them; and these things are especially sacred. This should challenge us to give to him sacramentally, so that even our gifts of mere money for his kingdom can convey something of ourselves to him.

But faithfulness in stewards is not to be limited to church attendance or church giving. St. Paul also says, "Whatever ye do, do all for the glory of God." (Col. 3:17)

So stewardship is more than giving *money*, it is giving time and skills and prayer and thought to the church. It is more than giving to the church; it is giving to all the good causes that will help bring in the kingdom of God. It is more than *giving* money; it is also the way we earn our money and the ways we spend it. Good stewardship means budgeting our time and energy and attention; it means analyzing our life priorities and counting costs; it means being aware that some day we shall have to give an account of ourselves.

Worship and church giving are the start of a wider stewardship. If anyone needed proof that money is not everything, he could surely find it in the startling rise in juvenile delinquency. Parents, instead of sharing in their children's lives, instead of giving themselves to their children, gave them money, or schooling, or material things. Children "bought off" in this way easily felt unwanted or unloved. Just so, the giving of part of our time and part of our money cannot be a substitute for the giving of the rest of ourselves.

Christ himself indicates that he can be found, and be served, outside of the Church as well as inside. He is anyone who is hungry, or thirsty, or a stranger, or naked, or sick, or in prison. (Matt.25:40) Stewardship means realizing that there are some contributions only you can make to the household of God. For example, when our Lord enlisted Peter, he also got Peter's boat. A poor simple fisherman's working boat, crude and primitive and battered. And yet once it was the pulpit where Jesus preached one of his most important early sermons, one that produced four disciples. (Luke 5:3) That little boat was also the means of his escape from Herod the Tetrarch. (Matt. 14:13) If that boat had not been given, the Gospels might have told a different story. And whenever you or I withhold something that you or I should have given to the purpose of God, then Church history will some day tell a different story.

Jesus Christ is the great example of stewardship in his giving of himself to us. He is the foundation of this household of faith. Some of the great stewards of this household we know, and we call them saints. The outline of this house is the shadow of their greatness in self-giving. There are many others we don't know. Their giving of their lives and their spirit gives this house its life and its spirit. There have been hundreds of thousands of them. And there also have been many, perhaps hundreds, of good stewards here in our own parish, who gave this particular house of God in this place its outer fabric and its inner strengths. In all this process, great as it is, anyone who could have helped and failed to do so was badly missed. And that is true today as well; and true even of you and me. There is an old fable about our Lord meeting with some angels after his ascension. They asked, "What about your kingdom on earth now? What is your plan?" He looked at his disciples, a few dazed, simple men, slowly walking back to Jerusalem to face the Herodians, the Roman Empire, the whole world. He said, "Well, I have my disciples." The angels said, "But what if they fail you? What is your plan then?" He said, "I have no other plan."

Thomas B. Kennedy

Few people in the Church traveled more miles than Loren Mead during the Project Test Pattern days. Loren told me that the best stewardship sermon he had heard in those travels was one preached by Tom Kennedy in Boston. When visiting Trinity Parish to hear my old friend Thom Blair preach, I sought out Tom Kennedy at the coffee hour and asked him to send me the sermon. He did, and it does justice to John Coburn's comment, "Tom was one of our prize products from the Episcopal Theological Seminary."

Give and Forgive

THERE ARE TWO WORDS that I am going to talk about today. They are "give" and "forgive." Both are verbs. Both imply an action; action I hope that will come from you and me. Though one does not directly relate to the other, they are actions which have as a common root the fact that they depend upon a decision that is made with the heart as well as the mind. They are words that command our attention if we take seriously our presence in this place—children of God in his Church. First, let me speak about the verb give.

I

The Random House Dictionary of the English Language defines the verb "give" in the following way: "to present voluntarily and without expecting compensation; bestow." This is one of the reasons why we are here today: to give our offering—a monetary gift, to be exact—to present it voluntarily to the work of the Church for the coming year. We do so for many reasons, not the least of which is that the Church needs your gift. Not just your gift of money, but most importantly the giver of that money, *you*.

Let me make a few comments about giving. First, we do not talk about money very often. Yet at almost every service in this church an offering is received. It is there, but we do not talk about it. Jesus did talk about it. It was an important part of the lives of people in the first century. It is an important part of our lives now. Yet when Jesus talked about money it was done to dramatize something more important than money itself. Think of the parable that was read this morning, about Jesus' comment of giving to Caesar that which belongs to him and to God that which belongs to him. Thus, this morning we have to remember that giving money is important, but behind that giving is something much more important than mere cash.

We have to remember that when we give our money, we also give ourselves. Our money is tangible evidence that we care for the Church. Money is one of the tangible ways we have to measure the quality of our lives. For too many people in our society today, it is the only measure. I feel sorry for them. For we know that grace, beauty, humility, patience, faith, hope are qualities of life that none of us can do without if we are to truly live. Yet money is one thing we can all give to the Church that can express how we feel about those other qualities of our life. So we give money. I cannot tell you how much to give, whether it be a dollar or a thousand dollars. Only you can decide on that. But I can say that when you give, you should expect to give more than just cold cash. And without expecting any compensation.

Another comment about giving might be made in terms of asking a question. Why give at all? The best answer I know for that question came from Jesus: he said that it is more blessed to give than to receive. When you give in this context, you are the recipient. Sounds strange, but it is true. You give and you are blessed. You share in God's grace—pure and simple.

One of the most remarkable men I have ever known is the Reverend John D. Verdery, the headmaster of the Wooster School, a school I attended as a boy. He says that giving is fun; that is why most people give to his school, and being blessed is something we all enjoy. He must know a lot of people who are blessed because he has raised millions of dollars from over 12,000 separate givers. And John Verdery is one of the most blessed persons I know because he has given so much of himself to that school. I think that we can say the same for ourselves, that we feel better when we give than when we receive. To give is to be blessed; not to give is to fall short of the mark: God's grace.

Let us look at another example. Once again we turn to Jesus. He gave to us the only possession he had. He had no money, no family inheritance of cash value, no weekly or monthly income. But he did possess one thing that meant more to him than anything else: he had his own life. He gave it to us freely, without any strings attached. He bestowed it upon us, and he was blessed.

To me that is the perfect example of giving, and I daresay almost everyone of us here falls short of that mark. While his life was the perfect gift, our giving now acknowledges that perfection and allows us to share in the new life that he has bestowed upon us. Thus, we are here today to give. It is more blessed to give than to receive.

II

The second verb I want to talk to you about is "forgive." The New Testament lesson we read this morning also has to do with forgiveness. The author of that passage was probably discussing the way the early Church should exercise its power. Whether Jesus actually uttered these exact words to Peter is an issue for scholars to debate. That debate is not my concern this morning. The context in which they are written, though, may well represent how Jesus felt about forgiveness and its role in the life of the Church as well as for individual Christians. Forgiveness was something that the early Church could not ignore if they were to follow Jesus. Peter asked the question, "Lord, how often shall my brother sin against me and I forgive him? As many as seven times?" Jesus said to him, "I do not say to you seven times, but seventy times seven." What then follows is the parable of the unforgiving servant.

This passage in Matthew is often discussed in the context of trying to figure out arithmetically how many times one is to forgive his brother. In this case forgiveness is beyond calculation; it must come from the heart. Forgiveness is not just a state of mind, but an action that absolves the guilty of the sin he or she has committed.

Jesus seemed to be telling Peter the following: If *you* are unable to forgive, God is, in turn, unable to forgive you. That is very simple and straightforward. "If you forgive . . . your heavenly Father will also forgive you." (Matt. 6:14) God's forgiveness and man's are inextricably interwoven, for one is dependent upon the other.

Let us look briefly at forgiveness in light of the individual. We are not saying that we are to forget about the law. If a man robs me, I do not just say, "You are forgiven. Go and steal no more." We do have an obligation to support and enforce the law as it concerns stealing. But at the same time we do not prosecute with vengeance, but rather with forgiveness, foregiveness that comes, not from the law or the head but from the heart. We are both children of God, and under the law of Christ I will forgive him as many times as he sins against me. This is what leads to a new relationship in God's kingdom.

Let us now look at forgiveness in terms of the Church. To recognize the need for forgiveness is to acknowledge the fact

that there is sin in the world. One of the peculiar events that
has occurred in our society today is our failure to admit that
sin exists. The word is rarely used any more. Sociologists will
talk about people being victims of their environment, or
psychiatrists will explain someone's antisocial behavior as de-
stuctive or aggressive, depending upon whether he is hurting
himself or others. The word sin is never used. I suppose to
use the word sin implies some kind of moral judgment.
However, I agree with the supposition that Karl Menninger
makes in his new book, *What Ever Became of Sin?* He says that
the word sin has disappeared from our vocabulary and this is
symbolic of what is partially remiss with our society today.
Dr. Menninger, a noted and renowned psychiatrist, says that
since 1952, when Congress required the President of the
United States to proclaim each year a national day of prayer,
the word sin has been used just once. That was in 1953 when
President Eisenhower borrowed the words from the procla-
mation used by President Lincoln in 1863. Neither the Demo-
crats nor the Republicans have used the word since. They
have skirted the word by referring to the problems of "pride"
and "self-righteousness." So, as a nation, we officially ceased
from sinning some twenty years ago!

I do not want to dwell on this point any longer except to say
that as a nation, as a people, as individuals we all need to forgive and to be forgiven. This implies that we have trans-
gressed the law of God, we have failed to do as we should
have toward our brother. I think we all know that to be true.

III

One of the missions of the Church, whether it be here in Copley Square in the Diocese of Massachusetts or in the National
Church, is to acknowledge man's transgressions before God
and to offer forgiveness and reconciliation. At times the
Church has forgotten that mission. It has been the transgres-
sor rather than the reconciler.

The Church is by no means perfect, because you and I are that Church—and I know that I am not perfect. I know I need God's forgiveness, and the only way I can receive that is in the act of forgiving my brother, no matter how many times he has sinned against me.

The Church, then, needs God's forgiveness, but it can only receive it when the Church itself forgives. Let us think about this for a moment. In order to forgive our brother, we have to take some action. It is the same with the Church. Forgiveness involves more than just saying, "I forgive you." It involves saying to your brother, "In God's eyes we are all equal, we are all the same." By offering forgiveness we remove the barriers that separate us as persons. This leaves open the possibility of grace.

Forgiveness in and of itself means very little. But put in the context of Jesus' life, it means we have the obligation not only to forgive but to bring about reconciliation and healing. This is the mission of the Church; and not its only mission but a significant and vital part of its work if God's forgiveness is to be bestowed upon it.

This is the responsibility of our ministry here in Copley Square. It is providing adequate housing for those who do not have it. It is working with the lost and lonely and forgotten whether they be young, middle-aged, or elderly. It is providing and maintaining a place such as this building, a refuge from the storms of life, a place that may give hope and a vision of our life together through the music and prayers. It is a place where we come to forgive and to be forgiven.

The ministry may be performed by the diocese to those who are in prisons or on welfare, or to those who are victims of man's inhumanity to man. Or it may be our college chaplains attempting to make their institutions responsible for the moral and ethical implications of their research and teaching. The task is unlimited. Even our National Church, through a special program designed to help empower people— particularly blacks, Spanish-speaking, Indians, and Eskimos—that they may for the first time in their lives have some control over their destiny. Our responsibility for ministry to these people should not diminish. Our action must not be curtailed. We must be more vigilant.

In conclusion let me say this. It would be easier to retreat to our comfortable havens rather than weather the storms of injustice, immorality, racism, or man's transgressions against God. But God has called us to forgive, and we cannot retreat. Forgiveness is a beneficent invasion, not an invasion such as was done on the beaches of Normandy in World War II, but rather like the invasion of the love that comes over a mother with her child, or that of two lovers. It is alert, it is patient, it is creative. It can at times shake you to your foundations and make you a new person.

The Church does collectively what you and I could never do individually. It sets before others in this broken world—be it this community, this state, this nation—the mission of forgiveness and reconciliation. During this present period of our personal and national history, when we seem to be recognizing more than ever the brokenness of life, the transgressions we have made against our neighbor and thus against God, we need the action of forgiveness and reconciliation that is rooted in our hearts, not just in our lives.

I stated at the beginning that the verbs "give" and "forgive" are not directly related. However, they become interwoven when we put them and ourselves within the context of the Church. Only by our giving both our money and ourselves can the Church continue with its mission of forgiveness. Only when we forgive can God forgive us. Let us give and forgive, for then we will be blessed and forgiven, the true measure of God's grace.

F. Reid Isaac III

Reid Isaac, son of a Methodist minister, has had a varied career in service to the Christian community. Reid headed a Congregational mission in the slums of East London, served as coordinator of the Youth Division of Christian Education on the Episcopal Church Center staff, on the staff of the Bishop of New York, and as an editor-in-chief of The Seabury Press. He has authored a curriculum for the United Church of Christ and the book, What's God Doing Today? *When Reid and I were co-workers in the Episcopal Church Center, I persuaded him to contribute this sermon—which I had heard praised— to this book. Since then Reid has returned to the parish because of his continuing and very strong belief that "the parish is viable because that's where the people are."*

Why Pledge?

While we have time, let us do good unto all men; and especially unto them who are of the household of faith.

Galatians 6:10

THIS IS the time of year when many parishes and missions ask their members to pledge money to support work for the coming year. Americans are used to being asked for money.

We know that every institution not paid for by taxes or foundations regularly appeals to its constituency for financial support. We know that each appeal tells us that more is needed than was received last year, and that without our help the program will not go on.

Each of us has to evaluate many such appeals for our support. We have to decide, "How important is this cause to me? What difference would it make if this project closed up?" Each person who is approached to support the Church must ask the same questions. What is it that we are supporting when we give money to the Church, and how important is it to us?

The offertory sentences used in many churches suggest that gifts to the Church are gifts to the poor.

> To do good, and to distribute, forget not; for with such sacrifices God is well pleased.
> Whoso hath this world's good, and seeth his brother have need, and shutteth up his compassion from him, how dwelleth the love of God in him?
> And the King shall answer and say unto them, Verily I say unto you, Inasmuch as ye have done it unto one of the least of these my brethren, ye have done it unto me.

But as a matter of fact, most of the money we put in the offering plates goes to pay salaries of Church staff, the oil company for heat, contractors for repairs, crayons for Sunday School, and to supply a house for the bishop. Very little of what we give goes to the poor. The time we give money to the poor is when we pay our taxes, not on Sunday morning.

In biblical times when the faithful were asked to give ten percent of their income to God, the religious institutions were the primary agencies for helping the poor. This is no longer the case. Today we help the poor by paying taxes and participating in politics to help determine how the taxes will be spent.

When we are approached to make a gift for the support of the Church, the money is not going to support programs for the poor, primarily, but to keep alive a particular religious institution. It is time that we talked directly about the importance of this institution to us and to our society.

As the influence of the Church in our culture declines, as social pressure to support it financially decreases, as the cause of Christianity becomes less popular, and as cultural pressures to support the Church lessen, each of us must ask himself with new seriousness, "How much am I committed to this, really? Why should I give?"

Here are some answers for one man. They may or may not be the answer for you. But for one person, this is what his commitment means.

He supports the Church because it is one institution in the community in the business of bringing people of all ages together in the search for meaning and value in life. He wouldn't be interested in a church that had all the answers and could hand them to him in a neat package. He would be interested in a community that gives him a chance to search. He would like to find and support a community that knows what questions men are asking about life and its meaning, and that creates an atmosphere where those questions could be honestly faced. If the parish church provided such an opportunity for him and his children, he would eagerly support it.

Secondly, he supports the parish church because it preserves and uses a tradition of poetry, song, worship, and theology that has a dignity and breadth, a height and depth, against which the experiences of his life can be seen. The parish is a place where his child is declared to be God's child and welcomed as part of a family stretching across the centuries. The parish is a place where he is reminded week after week that bread and wine are sacred bearers of the divine life. The parish is a place where a man and a woman can promise to love, comfort, honor, and keep each other in sickness and in health, and where they can confess together their failure to do what they have promised. The parish is a place where the death of his family, his friends, and ultimately of himself is felt and noticed and set within the context of God's eternity.

The parish is a place where the Christian story is told and retold. It's an absurd story about how the creator of the world did something spectacular with a Galilean carpenter that said

"Love" so loud that we can still hear the echoes. The heart of the Christian faith, the sublimely simple nub of it, is that the darkness that surrounds us, and toward which we travel, hides the outstretched arms of a loving God. If the retelling of that story ceases on earth, it will be a crueler place and a place with less hope in it. So he will continue to support the institution where the ancient story is told again and again, because in this dark world we can use all the hope we can get.

Finally, he supports the Church in order to strengthen the Christian voice in the affairs of the city, the nation, and the world. He wants to support that voice and that influence most of all when it disturbs him and judges him and hauls him up out of his indifference, blindness, and selfishness. For a Church that would only comfort him and never challenge him is only a tranquilizer or an aspirin. He is too big for that, and the world is too big for that. He wants to support the Church in these times particularly because it is an institution made up of all sorts and conditions of men, not his kind of men only. The Church's voice is currently being heard, and the Church's money is currently being spent on behalf of those people whom he has not heard from or cared about enough in the past. He is glad when his Church risks money to support the aspirations of the oppressed. Very little of what he gives goes for that purpose, but the part that does says a lot on his behalf.

These are one man's reasons for giving to a parish church. It is one of the few institutions designed to put the search for meaning and value at the top of its agenda. It provides a set of traditions, ceremonies, and symbols without which we would be poorer in meeting the crises of our own lives. The story it has to tell about a God who loved the world and gave himself for it in Jesus Christ must not be forgotten. The voice of the Church in our cities and our country is a reconciling voice, even though it disturbs us; and we must learn to trust it more because it is not afraid to disturb us.

These are some of the reasons the Church has a claim on our money and our lives.

W. David Crockett

"Davy" Crockett is one of the best known diocesan stewardship trainers in the northeastern United States. His published workbook, Sound Financial Stewardship *(New York: Morehouse-Barlow, 1973) is in use throughout the Church.*

After the First Province workshop, Canon Crockett wrote, "Your introduction and the four presentations were worth the price of admission! If the participants had ears to hear, they were getting the real thing. Even though I have been heavily involved in stewardship teaching for twenty years, I came away with some new ideas for promotion and training."

We are delighted to have one of the many Crockett sermons on stewardship as a part of this book.

Grace, Freedom and Stewardship

I UNDERSTAND that in ancient Rome it was absolutely impossible for a slave to purchase his own emancipation. It just could not be done. Freedom could be neither purchased nor earned because this sort of thing was forbidden by law. Freedom was a gift which could only be given—freely given. The owner of a slave merely had to point his finger at him and say one single word. That word was *gratia*.

How interesting it is to note that from this same Latin word *gratia*(free), we derive the word "grace." "Grace" and "free" are somehow totally intertwined. It is doubly interesting to me today because here I am in Grace Church.

Grace has come to mean the will of God (which is his love) as active on behalf of mankind, and actually operative within man himself. It is both outward and inward all at the same time.

In trying to define this word "grace" for Confirmation classes, I used to say, "Grace is the love of God in action."

Grace is not a passive thing at all. Rather, it is always active. It has to be in movement either on a vertical plane or a horizontal plane or it just is not grace. A recognition that all we have (this is why we say a grace before meals), all that we are (there but for the grace of God go I), and all that we hope to be (filled with God's grace and heavenly benediction) is given to us. It is, as it were, God pointing a finger at us and saying, *"Gratia."*

The gift of divine love, graciously given by God to his creatures, is the enabler which makes it possible for you and me to keep in a proper relationship with him and with our fellow creatures. And, God willing, to advance toward sanctity.

God has given freely of his love—that is, grace—and nothing we have done, or that mankind has ever done, has either earned or deserved that love. On the contrary, history, both secular and ecclesiastical, is replete with examples of our unworthiness. Yet, grace abounds more and more because it is of the very nature of God who creates, sustains, and sanctifies.

Believe me, it is only through the grace of God that you or I can do that which is right. This is a gift, and it is totally undeserved. We have been chosen by grace, and it is only through this gratuitous gift that we are free—free to choose the right from the wrong. It is only through this gift of grace that we have any hope of overcoming our natural inclinations to do the wrong. It is only through God's love in action that I am able to hold up my head above my failures, and to have a sense of being free. It is God who has said *"Gratia"* to me.

Grace is not opposed to our human wills, but actually acts through our wills. When the finger of God touches us, then we are operating within the sphere of grace, and here is the only place that true freedom is found. Were it not for grace, we would not be merely wallowing in our failures—the things that we have done and the things we have left undone—but we would be swallowed up by them. Grace has freed us from the mire.

Although grace can be neither earned nor bought, the means of grace are at hand and can be appropriated. Every confirmed person knows that the definition of a sacrament is: An outward and visible sign of an inward and spiritual grace. And we should all know that the sacraments are the very means whereby we can receive grace. Through the sacraments, the love of God is in action inwardly, and this is grace. How this may be operative is a mystery and, like all other spiritual mysteries, can only be experienced.

All I know is that through the grace of God I was incorporated into the body of Christ by Holy Baptism; by the gift of God I was strengthened in Holy Confirmation; by the sacrifice of Jesus Christ I am enabled, through Holy Communion, to be indwelt by his spirit; by God's love in action I can dwell in Holy Matrimony with my wife; by the reception of Holy Unction I am healed in body and soul; by the cross my sins are forgiven in Holy Penance; and I am enabled by a gracious God to function in Holy Orders as a priest.

None of these are deserved, none are earned, none are of my doing. All are freely given gifts of a loving God who has said "*Gratia.*"

Now, the first purpose in any stewardship program is to teach us something about the sovereignty of God, his graciousness, and what our response to this ought to be. We believe that everything comes from God. Matter and energy are uniquely his, and they are component parts of everything else. You and I cannot create them. All we can do is use them and manipulate them to our own purposes. God has given us this freedom. Our time, our abilities, and all of our possessions are derived from his gratuitous gifts. Without this inheritance from the creator, we would be nothing.

Through Jesus Christ—God Incarnate—you and I have entered into a wondrous relationship with the creator of all things. God, who is king of all, became one of us for a brief time so that we might know this relationship. It is not a relationship of master and slaves because he has, as it were, pointed his finger at us and made us free. Rather it is a relationship of father and children. It is the relationship of a father who has entrusted all of his goods to us and calls upon us to continue his work. Because we have been engrafted into the body of Christ through our Baptism, we are called upon to do his work during our brief stay in this world.

The second purpose of a stewardship program is to teach us how to properly use God's gracious gifts. We are but stewards of these for a time, and are to remember that at all times they belong to him. And to him we will have to give an accounting. This means one hundred percent of our treasure! If a stewardship program will help to teach us this, then we will be in good shape. Our accountability is not for one, two, five or ten percent of God's gifts, but for the full measure. If we take the stewardship message seriously, we will be devoting a portion of the freely given inheritance we have received from God to forward his work. We will do so in thankfulness for that which we have received.

Now, isn't it interesting to note that the Latin word *gratia,* which means "free," and is also the derivation of the word "grace," becomes, in both Spanish and Italian, the word for "thanks"? Believe me, they are all tied in together.

God has made us free. He has freely given us of his creation, and this personal favor of God, which we call grace, also calls upon us to respond in thanks-giving.

A third purpose for a stewardship program is to insure our own development. If we accept our responsibilities as stewards and do give thankfully of our time, our abilities, and our treasure to do God's work in this community,·in his world, and in the Church which is uniquely his creation, then we grow in faith and hasten his kingdom.

Let me try to be more specific. The Lord has commanded his followers to love God and to love their neighbors. Like freedom and grace, these are so tied up with one another that

they cannot be separated. A program of Christian stewardship is designed to underscore the meaning of grace and to
promote an outpouring of our love.

Let's take the Church first. We give thankfully of our time
in worship and prayer. We give thankfully of our abilities in
Christian service as priests, teachers, choir members, ador-
ners of the altar, acolytes, members of the vestry, and in
many other ways. We provide a place for worship which becomes a base for the spreading of God's word and the edifica-
tion of his people. Grace Church stands in this community as
an everlasting symbol that God cares and that we speak out
through it as his witnesses.

In this community we are called upon to do God's work by
giving thankfully of our God-given time, abilities, and treasure. Some heed this call, and others are so deafened by the
clamor of this world that they cannot hear Christ's call to
serve even as he served. Our hospitals, our schools, our civic
institutions all call for our help. These too belong to God and
are doing his work.

The alleviation of pain, hunger, misery, ignorance, and
want of any kind in this world beckons to us all. We who have
so very much must share that which we have with those less
fortunate than ourselves. World relief programs, the United
Way, the Presiding Bishop's Fund for World Relief, and many
others call us to demonstrate our love for our neighbor. In a
shrinking world, where transportation and communication
are so rapid, it becomes impossible for us to ignore need.
Perhaps this is why we frequently add the words, "and make
us ever mindful of the needs of others," to our mealtime
grace.

Jesus Christ commanded us to go teach all nations and to
baptize them "in the Name of the Father, and of the Son, and
of the Holy Spirit." This is our missionary imperative! Had
we even begun to meet this challenge, our world might be a
different place today. With the thankful giving of our time,
our abilities and our treasure we must redeem the mistakes
and failures of the past and move forward. We must do God's
work!

A few years ago we developed a program in our diocese which we called "Stewardship for the Seventies." Among our materials were a poster and bulletins bearing these words:

> Inflation hasn't changed the price of God's grace. It is still free.

A parish bearing the name Grace knows that God has freely given of his love and that it is still active and operative in his world. It knows that we have been made free in order that we may respond in thanks for his gifts.

Practice Christian stewardship and you will enter into a new appreciation of the sovereignty of Almighty God. Practice Christian stewardship and you will learn to use all of his gifts in thankfulness. Practice Christian stewardship and assure your own development in the sight of both God and man. Practice Christian stewardship and hasten his kingdom of love. It is a way of life. It falls within the realm of grace.